TITANIC

THE TRUTH BEHIND THE DISASTER

PETER THRESH

Crescent Books
New York

This 1992 edition published by
Crescent Books,
distributed by Outlet Book
Company, Inc.,
a Random House Company,
225 Park Avenue South,
New York, New York 10003

Produced by
Brompton Books Corporation
15 Sherwood Place,
Greenwich, CT 06830

ISBN 0-517-06699-8

8 7 6 5 4 3 2 1

Printed and bound in Hong Kong

For Deborah, Madrinella,
George, and Edith

Page 1: Scenes of
desperation as the
Titanic sinks.

Pages 2-3: The beautiful
profile of the ill-fated
liner.

Pages 4-5: The *Titanic* in
Southampton harbor.

CONTENTS

INTRODUCTION

R.M.S. TITANIC (COPYRIGHT)

A T 11.45 pm on Sunday 14 April 1912 the SS *Titanic* struck an iceberg off the coast of Nova Scotia. When she sank nearly three hours later she took with her 1522 of the 2227 passengers and crew on board. Among those lost were people from all walks of life who had availed themselves of the increasingly popular transatlantic passenger services. For the *Titanic* included in its passenger list not only some of the wealthiest members of the American subcontinent but also the poorest of Irish farmers anxious to make a fresh start in the New World. In fact the *Titanic* was really a microcosm of society, with each member on board stationed according to his position. Thus when on that clear April night a 300-foot hole was gouged in her side, contemporary society was exposed for all to see in miniature form.

The sinking of the 'greatest liner on earth' was unlike many other disasters in that men and women had time to react and to conduct themselves according to their true natures. In the hours before the final, deathly plunge a drama was enacted on her decks which re-

Top: The elegant lines of the *Titanic* in a contemporary postcard.

Above: The tiny sailing boat is included in this publicity view to emphasize the vast size of the Olympic-class steamers.

vealed man with his nature stripped bare. There were tales of heroism, tales of devotion to duty, tales of love and not a few of cowardice which fired the imagination of an incredulous public and continue to do so to this day.

Somehow the myth had spread that the *Titanic* was unsinkable. For, as her Captain had said some years before, 'navigation had gone beyond that sort of thing.' As the flagship of the White Star Line the *Titanic* had been designed with many of the latest safety features, and these had been inspected by the Board of Trade. Belief in technological development had become almost a religious faith. Thus when news came of the scale of the disaster, the press and public reacted with a mixture of incomprehension and disbelief. This soon gave way to feelings of anger and introspection: while specific parties had no doubt behaved either recklessly or carelessly in causing the collision it was felt that society as a whole should bear some of the blame. Man had overstretched himself and put too much confidence in his own technology.

Right: The increasingly popular North Atlantic shipping lanes.

Below: Contemporary publicity for the White Star Line.

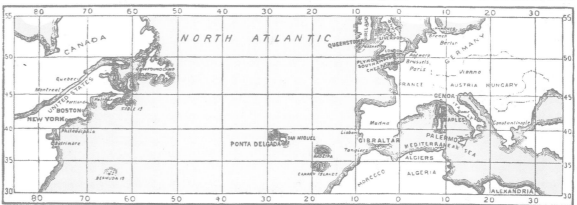

White Star Line United States & Royal Mail Steamers

WHITE STAR LINE

NEW YORK PLYMOUTH CHERBOURG SOUTHAMPTON	MONTREAL QUEBEC LIVERPOOL
NEW YORK QUEENSTOWN LIVERPOOL	NEW YORK AZORES MEDITERRANEAN
BOSTON QUEENSTOWN LIVERPOOL	BOSTON AZORES MEDITERRANEAN

United States & Royal Mail Steamers

Right: The *Olympic* sporting camouflage 'dazzle' paint and extra lifeboats during service in World War I.

After all, as the Bishop of Winchester said in his sermon the Sunday after the tragedy, the iceberg had a right to be there, man did not.

ATLANTIC TRAVEL

The *Titanic* and her two sister ships surpassed in scale and luxury anything imaginable even thirty years earlier. They were the result of a huge capital investment combined with developments in shipbuilding techniques. The motive for these developments was to be found in the enormous population growth in America. Between 1840 and 1890 the popu-

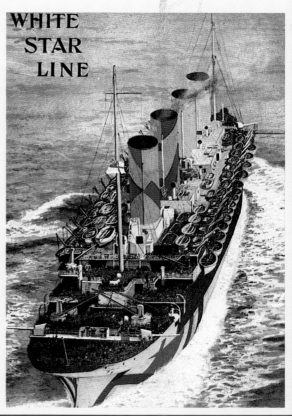

WHITE STAR LINE

7

lation of America had quadrupled, and with it there arose a huge demand for transatlantic travel. This demand came from all levels of society: from the poor hoping to find employment on the railroads; and from the rich who had made their fortunes opening up the continent and exploiting a burgeoning market.

America offered unprecedented opportunities for the amassing of huge wealth. Much of this was centered in the hands of the trusts and combines where huge capital was beginning to play a major part in the affairs of the shipping industry. One such combine was the Morgan Combine whose aim was to establish a monopoly on transatlantic travel similar to that enjoyed by others on the American railroads. The first target of the Morgan Combine was Cunard which for many years had been the rival of the White Star Line. As such they had been co-equals on the increasingly competitive transatlantic route. The injection of huge American capital into Cunard would, however, have dealt a death blow to White Star. They could not

hope to compete with Cunard on such terms.

Instead of competing with the Morgan Combine, White Star opted to join them. This important step was masterminded by W J Pirrie. He had come to occupy an increasingly paternalistic position in the affairs of White Star following the death of its autocratic founder, T H Ismay, in 1899. The Dictionary of National Biography credits him as 'the creator of the big ships.' An engineer – in an age when engineers were national heroes – and a shrewd businessman, Pirrie had built up the Harland and Wolff shipyard in Belfast so that by the turn of the century it was the largest in the world. It led the world in the development of hull designs and was more than ready to meet the increasing demands for larger ships.

This demand was fueled not only by the huge increase in the volume of traffic, but also in a demand for greater variety. Samuel Johnson had joked that 'Going to sea is like going to prison with the chance of being drowned,' but this kind of sentiment had at long last passed. First-class passengers now

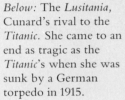

Below: The *Lusitania,* Cunard's rival to the *Titanic.* She came to an end as tragic as the *Titanic*'s when she was sunk by a German torpedo in 1915.

Above: The popular Café Parisien with its airy wicker-work informality.

expected luxury and this required space. Thus whereas the *Bothnia* had come into service in 1874 with a tonnage of 4555, by the turn of the century ships of three times that size were operating the transatlantic routes.

Between 1901 and 1907 White Star used Morgan Combine capital to commission four new ships: the *Celtic, Cedric, Baltic* and *Adriatic*, 'The Big Four' as they were known, were built at Harland and Wolff. They were capable of speeds of 16-17 knots and had a tonnage of between 21,000 and 24,000. Cunard responded with the *Lusitania* and *Mauretania* which, at 31,000 tons, were not only larger but also much faster. Cruising at 27-28 knots they reduced the crossing from a week to five days.

The threat posed by *Lusitania* and *Mauretania* formed the background to a meeting at Pirrie's Belgravia home in 1907. Over coffee and cigars Pirrie discussed with J B Ismay

(the son of T H Ismay) what response they would make in the face of the latest breed of Cunarders. Clearly it would be hopelessly uneconomic for White Star to compete against Cunard for speed since this would mean less space for passengers and cargo. Instead they decided to opt for a modest increase in their cruising speeds combined with an increase in size. The extra space would be used to attract passengers by providing special luxury for the rich and more spacious accommodation for the poor. Three compatible running mates were planned which were to have enabled White Star to operate a regular weekly service between England and New York. These were the *Olympic, Titanic* and *Gigantic* (renamed the *Britannic*). The loss of the *Titanic* as a member of this team, especially in such melodramatic circumstances, dealt the White Star line a body-blow from which it was never completely to recover.

THE CONSTRUCTION OF THE TITANIC

THE White Star response to the threat of the Morgan Combine had been discussed by Pirrie and J B Ismay over coffee and cigars in the sedate surroundings of Belgravia, but it is to the noise and sweat of the Harland and Wolff shipyard in Belfast that we must travel to see that response taking shape.

Harland and Wolff differed from other shipyards in two main respects. First, it was a shipyard which built not just the superstructures and hulls of the ships, but also most of the major machinery that went into them. Second, it operated on an unusual 'cost plus' relationship when building for White Star. This relationship was a testimony to the mutual trust and respect that had built up be-

tween Pirrie and the Ismays over the past twenty years. The arrangement guaranteed Harland and Wolff a satisfactory profit and enabled White Star to commission the very finest ships that could be built. Harland and Wolff could do its best work and make honest recommendations concerning construction without fear of being undercut by a rival. This was the basis on which Harland and Wolff was to build the three sister ships *Olympic, Titanic,* and *Gigantic.*

The dimensions of the new ships were astonishing. They were to be 883 feet in length and 92½ feet in beam and have a gross tonnage of 45,000. Their competitors, the existing Cunard giants *Lusitania* and *Mauretania,* were some ninety feet shorter,

Left: A 1914 White Star advertisement for its Transatlantic Service.

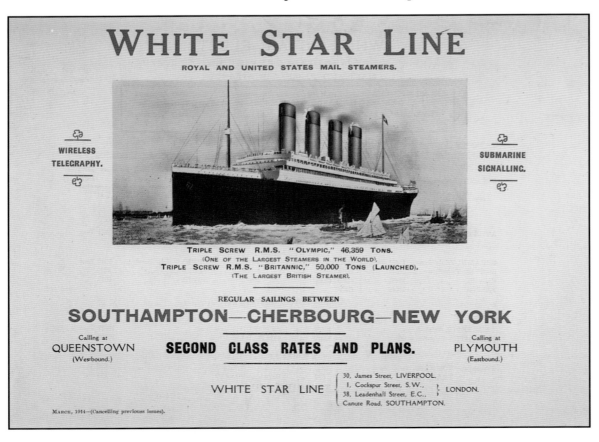

WHITE STAR LINE
ROYAL AND UNITED STATES MAIL STEAMERS.

WIRELESS TELEGRAPHY.

SUBMARINE SIGNALLING.

TRIPLE SCREW R.M.S. "OLYMPIC," 46,359 TONS.
(ONE OF THE LARGEST STEAMERS IN THE WORLD).
TRIPLE SCREW R.M.S. "BRITANNIC," 50,000 TONS (LAUNCHED).
(THE LARGEST BRITISH STEAMER).

REGULAR SAILINGS BETWEEN

SOUTHAMPTON—CHERBOURG—NEW YORK

Calling at
QUEENSTOWN
(Westbound.)

SECOND CLASS RATES AND PLANS.

Calling at
PLYMOUTH
(Eastbound.)

WHITE STAR LINE { 30, James Street, LIVERPOOL, 1, Cockspur Street, S.W., 38, Leadenhall Street, E.C., Canute Road, SOUTHAMPTON. } LONDON.

MARCH, 1914—(Cancelling previous issues).

Left: The hull of the *Britannic* nears completion.

four feet narrower, and 14,000 tons lighter. The first two of the three White Star liners planned to compete with the Cunarders were to be constructed side by side and launched within a year or so of one another.

The first problem for Harland and Wolff was that none of her slips was large enough to accommodate the behemoths being planned. Therefore three of the slips were combined to make two giant slips known as Samson and Goliath. A towering new gantry, the largest of its kind ever built, was erected to facilitate the construction of the ships. This gantry, dubbed the Great Gantry, was an impressive structure and photographs show that it dominated not only the shipyard but the city as well. The journalist and man of letters Filson Young described the yard as a

multitudinous clamour of thousands and thousands of blows of metal on metal coming from a veritable forest of iron . . . a multitude of Pigmy men swarming and toiling amid the skeleton iron structures.

The keel of the *Olympic* was laid down on 16 December 1908. She was launched on 20 October 1910 and completed in May 1911.

The *Titanic* was laid down on 31 March 1909, framed by April 1910, frame plated by October 1910 and launched on 31 May 1911. The *Olympic* and *Titanic* were in turn transferred from the gantry area to a new deep-

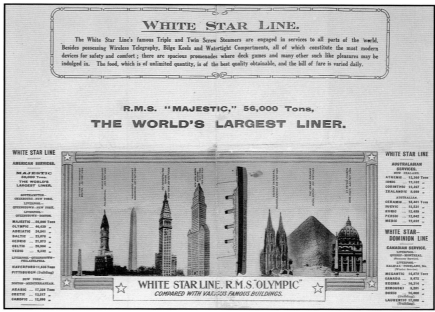

Above: The 883-foot *Olympic* compared with some of the world's tallest structures.

water wharf for fitting out. This work was done with the aid of a remarkable 200-ton floating crane and, in the *Titanic*'s case, took some ten months to complete.

Everything about the ships was on an epic scale. The rudders weighed 20,250 lbs, the anchors were as tall as a house, and the links in the chain were taller than a man. Three million rivets were driven home at the rate of 200 per day per squad. A squad consisted of four men working from six in the morning until half past five in the evening. The first

The hulls of the ship were made of inch-thick steel plate. Each hull had eight decks (lettered downwards as Boat Deck then A, B, C, D, E, F, and G). Below these were located the boiler rooms and holds. Two important safety features were incorporated in the design of the hull. First, a double bottom was constructed (in between which a man had enough space to walk). Although this did not extend above the water line it was unusual in that it was carried above the bilge instead of stopping short of it. Second, the hull was subdivided into sixteen watertight compartments by means of 15 half-inch thick bulkheads which extended up through the F Deck at the bow and stern and through the E Deck in the middle two thirds of the ship. Heavy watertight doors provided communication between the compartments during normal operation. These 'cylinder' doors, as they were known, could be closed in three ways: by means of an electric switch on the bridge, by a lever next to the door, and by an automatic trip device which sealed off that compartment in the event of any incoming water. The ship was designed to remain afloat with any two compartments flooded. Since the worst imagined scenario of a broadside collision would damage no more than two compartments at most the *Titanic* was generally regarded as practically unsinkable. Indeed

Above: Thomas Andrews, Major Archie Butt, and Lord Pirrie, controller of Merchant Shipbuilding in Great Britain.

Right: The *Titanic* nearing completion in the great gantry at Harland and Wolff.

Far right: Work starts on the massive iron-plate hull.

man (the heater boy) heated the rivet in a coke brazier for three to four minutes, threw it to a 'catch boy' who put the stall of the rivet into a hole through two overlapping plates. While a third man held it in position a fourth man flattened the rivet into the hole.

the British shipping trade journal the *Shipbuilder* described the *Olympic* as precisely that in its commemorative edition of 1911. The idea spread and the qualifier was lost. The *Shipbuilder* went on to describe the engines in some detail. In 1909 Harland and Wolff had come up with a novel three-prop design (tested on the *Laurentic*) that used two outboard reciprocating engines with a low-pressure turbine in the middle. This center turbine would be run off the excess steam cast off by the two-reciprocating engines. Twenty-nine huge boilers having 159 furnaces in all were needed to provide the steam for this machinery. This design combined comfortable cruising speeds of 21 knots with economy of operation.

Twenty lifeboats were fitted to the *Titanic* in case of emergencies. These consisted of sixteen regular wooden lifeboats and four Englehardt collapsibles. In 1910 the prevailing view was that lifeboats were needed to ferry passengers to rescue vessels sure to be waiting nearby in the crowded North Atlantic shipping lanes rather than for a total evacuation of the ship. A damaged ship was expected to stay afloat for hours or even days. Indeed the *Republic* did precisely that after it was involved in a collision on 23 January 1909 off Nantucket while en route for New York. All her passengers were rescued before she sank some thirty-eight hours later. It is against this background that one must con-

Above left: Publicity material for the White Star Line.

Top: A Jacobean-style first-class stateroom.

Above: An Empire-style first-class suite.

sider the question of the woefully inadequate provision of lifeboats on the *Titanic*.

Alexander Carlisle, managing director of Harland and Wolff until 1910, had originally proposed 64 lifeboats for the *Titanic*. This number was later reduced to 32 after his retirement. White Star, however, rejected that idea, electing instead to remain within the Board of Trade regulations. These required simply that ships of more than 10,000 tons should carry 16 lifeboats. To have provided a greater lifeboat capacity on all Olympic-class ships would be expensive not only for the ships of that class but would also have made other White Star ships appear to have been underequipped, necessitating a costly upgrading at a time when White Star faced the strongest possible competition on the North Atlantic route. In their defense it should be pointed out that there was not a single large liner on the North Atlantic with anything like enough boats to handle the evacuation of all passengers and crew. Clearly the Board of Trade had been slow to respond to the problems posed by the ex-

pansion of Atlantic liners in under 2 decades from 10,000 to 46,000 tons; the *Republic* incident mentioned above was hardly likely to quicken their step. Indeed the incident probably lulled the shipping community into an even greater sense of security since help had been summoned by the relatively new means of the wireless.

Since its provision on the Royal Yacht in 1898 the use of Marconi's apparatus had spread rapidly, until by 1912 hundreds of ships were carrying wireless machines.

Above: The magnificent smoking room.

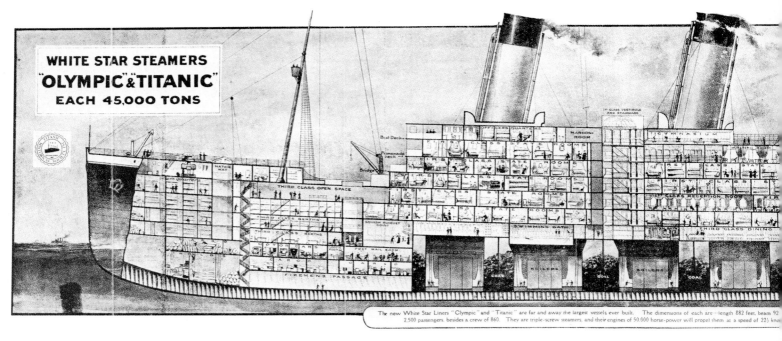

WHITE STAR STEAMERS
"OLYMPIC" & "TITANIC"
EACH 45,000 TONS

The new White Star Liners "Olympic" and "Titanic" are far and away the largest vessels ever built. The dimensions of each are—length 882 feet, beam 92
2,500 passengers, besides a crew of 860. They are triple-screw steamers, and their engines of 50,000 horse-power will propel them at a speed of 22½ knots

Above: A cross-section of the *Titanic* showing the disposition of facilities, passengers, and crew.

Right: The massive reciprocating engines in the Harland and Wolff workshop, Belfast.

Far right: A view from the quay showing Captain Smith (top) and a lifeboat.

Using Marconi transmitters and receivers, the operators in the Marconi rooms on board ships in the North Atlantic could communicate with and through each other to the large ring of receiving stations on the North American coast, most notably Cape Race. The *Titanic* was equipped with just such a Marconi room near to the bridge and had a powerful transmitter with three separate power supplies. It was not inappropriate that her chief wireless operator became a posthumous hero of the disaster, sending out distress calls until the very last moment.

While specialists and those of a technical bent were, no doubt, intrigued by the various elements of the ship's construction, it was the way in which these engineering advances met the needs and requirements of the passengers which attracted custom to the White Star line.

Passenger Accommodation

It is probably fair to say that the passengers of 1850 would scarcely have recognized the liners of 1900, such were the advances made in ship design. The *Oceanic* of 1899 had set a standard of luxury for liners of the future, the crowning glory of which would be the giant trio of the *Olympic, Titanic,* and *Gigantic.* This Olympic class of liner was certainly the

finest built in terms of Edwardian elegance and sophistication in the first-class accommodation. But in the second and even third classes very considerable improvements were made over similar accommodation offered by other liners. The White Star Olympic-class liners were designed to con-

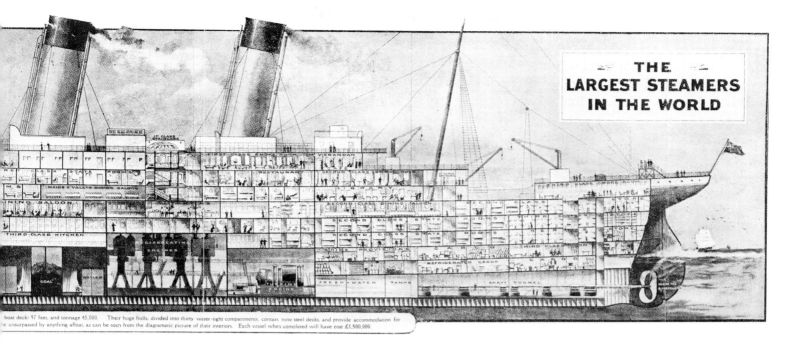

THE LARGEST STEAMERS IN THE WORLD

boat deck) 97 feet, and tonnage 45,000.   Their huge hulls, divided into thirty water-tight compartments, contain nine steel decks, and provide accommodation for re unsurpassed by anything afloat, as can be seen from the diagramatic picture of their interiors.   Each vessel when completed will have cost £1,500,000

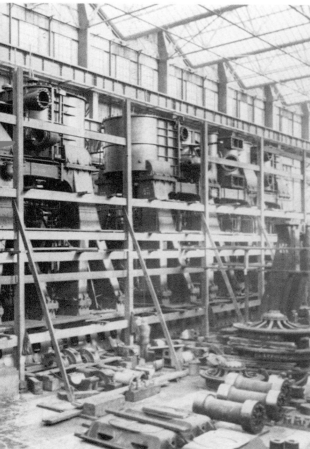

vey the passenger across the Atlantic 'with the speed and certainty of an Express train.'

The *Olympic* and *Titanic* were designed to accommodate 2345 passengers and a crew complement of about 860. The passenger capacity was divided between 689 first class, 674 second class and 1026 third class. While minor differences existed between the *Titanic* and the *Olympic*, it is important to remember that they were designed and fitted out at sister-ships. Indeed White Star made no distinction in its advertising material between the two.

The first-class quarters occupied the whole of the ship between the four funnels and were designed to resemble a ship as little as possible. Everything which could have reminded one that one was aboard a ship was carefully hidden from view beneath panelling and tapestries so that, as the *Liverpool Daily Post* stated, the ships were 'the Hotel Cecil afloat.'

The *Shipbuilder* outlined the quarters thus:

The first-class public rooms include the dining saloon, reception room, restaurant, lounge, reading and writing room, smoking room and the verandah cafés and palm courts. Other novel features are the gymnasium, squash court, Turkish and electric baths and the swimming bath. Magnificent suites of rooms and cabins of sizes and styles sufficiently diverse to suit the likes and dislikes of any passenger are provided. There is also a barber's shop, a dark room for photographers, a clothes pressing room, a special dining room for maids and valets, a lending library, a telephone system and a wireless telegraphy installation. Indeed, everything has been done in regard to the furniture and fittings to make the first-class accommodation more than equal to that provided in the finest hotels on shore.

The *Shipbuilder* was a serious trade publication not given to hyperbole and in its factual account scarcely does justice to the scale and extent of the luxury. Sir Philip Gibbs was more lyrical:

All that the genius of modern life has invented for comfort and adornment was lavished upon her in a prodigal spirit; all that wealth and art can attain in splendour was given to her decoration. The imagination of old story tellers writing of fabulous ships paled before the actuality of this magnificence . . . English gentlemen might sit in rooms panelled and adorned like those of Haddon Hall, and fair women might have their beauty reflected in oval mirrors hanging upon walls like those of Versailles when Marie Antoinette played with her ladies.

Even Sir Philip, however, fails to describe the extraordinary opulence of the best cabins. For even in first class there existed different levels of splendor. This was especially so for the *Titanic* since the promenade on the Bridge Deck (B Deck) had been forsaken in favor of the creation of 28 new staterooms and suites, two of which even enjoyed their own promenade.

Left: The first-class dining saloon catering for 500 diners.

Above: The oak-paneled second-class smoking room.

Below left: A first-class 'Regence' suite.

The special staterooms located amidships on B and C Deck were executed in a dazzling variety of styles. The passengers in these accommodations could choose from any of the following designs: Louis XIV, XV, XVI, Empire, Italian Renaissance, Georgian Regence (Regency), Queen Anne, and both Modern and Old Dutch. Some of them had Adam fireplaces that burned coal in their sitting rooms and double four-poster beds in the bedrooms. The most costly suites were the four parlor suites which consisted of a sitting room, two bedrooms, two wardrobe rooms, a private bath, and a lavatory. The other suites consisted of two staterooms joined by an interconnecting door.

The ordinary first-class staterooms, although more modest, were a far cry from what had prevailed half a century earlier. All had washbasins and some their own baths. While some were single-berth rooms, others were arranged for up to three people – two in twin beds and one in an upper berth that lowered when required. In short, the range of rooms in first class was such that as many as possible would be attracted to that class of travel. But it was not the staterooms alone

which enticed the passengers. For to travel first class entitled one to the many other attractions on offer in the public rooms.

A geographical point of reference for first-class passengers was provided by the grand stairway. This was done in a somewhat eclectic late-17th-century William-and-Mary style with a contemporary Louis XIV balustrade thrown in for good measure. It was located between the first two funnels and extended over six decks from the lower landing to the boat deck where it was lit by a huge glass and wrought iron dome. Presiding over this magnificent staircase were the two bronze figures, symbolizing Honor and Glory crowning Time in the form of a clock.

An important social hub of the ship was the dining saloon located on the D Deck. As Sir Philip Gibbs pointed out, this was modeled on the early seventeenth-century Jacobean style of Haddon Hall in Hatfield, England. Measuring 114 feet in length and 92 feet in width it was the largest such room on any liner and could serve 500 passengers at a sitting. A substantial reception room done in the same style in which one might greet one's guests adjoined the dining saloon. But first-class passengers could dine elsewhere if they so wished, for a separate first-class restaurant was provided on the Bridge Deck in which passengers might dine à la carte in more intimate surroundings for the payment of a supplement. As the *Engineer* observed, to dine in such a manner was 'more consonant with modern ideas as to diet.' The first-class restaurant had been introduced on the *Olympic* and was found to be immensely popular.

A larger restaurant was therefore designed for the *Titanic* and, for the first time, a Café Parisien complete with French waiters.

A meeting place for first-class passengers during the day time was the Lounge which was located on the Promenade Deck. This incorporated the paneling and ornament copied from the Palace of Versailles to which Sir Philip Gibbs alluded. Adjoining this was a Georgian reading and writing room for the

ladies. The men repaired to the smoking room located further back on the same deck. The walls of the smoking room were paneled in mahogany and inlaid with mother-of-pearl. A painting hung above the fireplace. Immediately aft the smoking room were the less-formal Mediterranean Palm Courts furnished in wicker.

The Olympic-class ships were notable for their sense of space and openness. The *Titanic* enjoyed two first-class promenades on the Promenade and Boat Decks. Respectively these were 500 and 200 feet in length. Away from the promenades the first-class passengers could exercise on the electric horse and camel in the gym or experiment with a novel feature of transatlantic life: a squash court (on G Deck) and a swimming pool measuring 30 feet by 14 feet (on F Deck). *Engineering* felt that the latter should appeal particularly to passengers since 'it is arranged much on the lines of an ordinary swimming bath on land and is fitted with dressing boxes and freshwater sprays.' Also on F Deck were to be found the Turkish and electric baths. They were decorated, according to the *Shipbuilder*,

Left: The *Titanic* is fitted out.

Above: The *Titanic*'s center anchor.

21

Right: Two of the three propellor shafts.

Below right: The hooters sound at 6 pm at Harland and Wolff.

Below: One of the fifteen watertight hydraulic doors.

in 'the Arabian style of the seventeenth century. The portholes are concealed by an elaborately carved Cairo curtain through which light fitfully reveals something of the grandeur of the mysterious East.'

The passengers in the second class did not have access to such grandeur. However the accommodation offered by White Star on the Olympic class of ships was of a standard similar to that of the first class of her competitors. The second-class area was situated to the rear of the ship and like the first class was arranged over seven decks linked by a grand stairway. An innovation for second-class passengers was the provision of an electric escalator. The second class enjoyed its own dining saloon, smoking room and library and ladies' room. Although less lavish than those of the first, the fittings and fixtures of the second-class accommodation were nonetheless stylish and elegant. Unknown to most passengers was the fact that the first- and second-class saloons shared the same galley which was certainly one of the most elaborate in existence. The saloon itself was 71 feet in length and paneled in oak in the Old English style. Here the passengers ate at long

tables – the norm for the period when at sea. After dinner the second-class passengers could retire to their oak-paneled smoking room or to the Colonial Adam-style sycamore-paneled library. The second-class staterooms were decorated in a simpler fashion than the first class but were of a similar size. They were designed to accommodate four people. As such they represented a considerable advance on what was offered by other lines. Exercise for second-class passengers could be taken on the promenade which was 145 feet in length.

Third-class passengers for their part were confined to a small promenade area on the Shelter Deck (C Deck) at the rear of the ship. Elsewhere space for these passengers was similarly reduced. Indeed the galley designed to cater for 1000 third-class passengers was actually smaller than the cooling room attached to the *Titanic*'s Turkish bath intended for perhaps a dozen or so first-class passengers. The third class had a dining saloon and a lounge called the General Room which was plainly fitted out in white enamel. Elsewhere there was a smoking room in paneled oak; but otherwise severe simplicity

was the order of the day. The third-class staterooms were situated in the less-desirable parts of the ship and in the lower decks and, while some could accommodate up to ten people, many were designed for only two or four passengers. This was a marked improvement over the traditional bunkhouse arrangements offered by most other lines. In this class White Star was offering transportation not luxury.

The crew of 860 men and officers was accommodated in the prow of the ship and on the Sun Deck. In short the ship was a microcosm of society with all accommodated according to their means and social position. Having described the accommodation available to them, we can now pass on to meet some of the passengers and crew and from there to the fateful journey itself.

THE SHIP'S COMPLEMENT

FIRST CLASS PASSENGER LIST

PER

ROYAL AND U.S. MAIL

S.S. "Titanic,"

FROM SOUTHAMPTON AND CHERBOURG
TO NEW YORK

(Via QUEENSTOWN).

Wednesday, 10th April, 1912.

Captain, E. J. Smith, R.D. (Commr. R.N.R.).
Surgeon, W. F. N. O'Loughlin.   Pursers { H. W. McElroy
Asst. Surgeon, J. E. Simpson.   { R. L. Barker.
Chief Steward, A. Latimer.

Allen, Miss Elizabeth   Andrews, Mr. Thomas
              Walton   Appleton, Mrs. E. D.

Allison, Mr. H. J.   Artagaveytia, Mr. Ramon

Allison, Mrs. H. J.   Astor, Colonel J. J.
   and Maid   and Manservant

Allison, Miss   Astor, Mrs. J. J.
                                  and Maid
Allison, Master
   and Nurse   Aubert, Mrs. N.
                                  and Maid
Anderson, Mr. Harry

Andrews, Miss Cornelia I.

Right: Colonel John Jacob Astor.

THAT those aboard the *Titanic* represented all sections of society cannot be doubted. For the *Titanic* had been constructed to take advantage both of the desire for incredible luxury among the transatlantic business class, who were willing to pay up to £870 for a one-way trip, and also for those able to spend only £2 for the journey and who were prepared to endure the relative inconvenience of a week aboard ship. For its maiden voyage the *Titanic* attracted a considerable amount of interest among the transatlantic aristocracy anxious to make the trip in style.

It was also the rich who attracted the most attention after the disaster for not only were they fabulously wealthy – representing a total capital of at least $600 million – but also they were interesting or eccentric characters in their own right. The name Colonel J J Astor would appear at the head of any list of passengers, for he was not only the wealthiest man on board the Titanic, but he was also someone who went down with the ship voluntarily. Astor was the evocative name that every newspaper sought in its headlines.

A photograph of the 47-year-old Astor dressed in his bowler hat and overcoat gives little hint of a fascinating character who, besides being fabulously wealthy (he was worth about $150 million), was enterprising and mildly eccentric. The great-grandson of a poor Swabian peasant emigrant, Astor had studied at Harvard and developed a keen interest in mechanical engineering. As 'the world's greatest monument to unearned increment' he could afford to indulge his passion for motor cars – picking up a speeding fine in Croydon – invention, and eccentricity while at the same time maintaining and extending the family's vast real-estate holdings

Mr. and Mrs. Isidor Strauss

Mr. Charles M. Hays

Mr. Henry B. Harris

Mr. J. B. Thayer

Above: A page from a memorial program showing prominent passengers.

Above right: Ben Guggenheim.

in New York. Assessed for tax just before his death, his Manhattan holdings alone amounted to 700 lots. Besides these activities Astor found time to invent and market a bicycle brake, a pneumatic device for flattening road surfaces, to experiment with new sorts of ship's turbines and to write an intriguing novel in which Colonel Bearwarden, President of the Terrestrial Axis Straightening Company, pumps out the Arctic to put the globe on an even keel. He was also a man of action. He financed his own units and fought in the Spanish-American war (hence the title Colonel). Besides this he was also an intrepid yachtsman – disappearing for sixteen days in his private yacht *Nourmahal* – only to reappear again unharmed.

But it was not so much these activities which fascinated the public as his matrimonial affairs.

In 1909 it was abruptly announced that Astor's wife had successfully sued him for divorce, all legal proceedings having been kept a secret, to the chagrin of the New York press. Two years later Astor resolved to marry an 18-year-old New York girl, Madeleine Force. Amid much controversy Astor persuaded a clergyman – who later resigned – to perform the ceremony. But he could not escape the prurient eyes of the press and society. Having tried unsuccessfully to escape the controversy on his yacht, he decided to take his young bride to Egypt for the winter, and from there to Paris and so back to the US aboard the *Titanic*.

Elsewhere in the list of first-class passengers one can find many men who represented the finest business brains in America, men who controlled vast industrial, commercial and financial concerns and whose names were household names. Chief among these was Benjamin Guggenheim. The son of an emigrant who began life in America in 1847 selling shoelaces in Philadelphia, Benjamin Guggenheim had inherited an immense fortune based on mining and smelting. The Guggenheim interests worth some $100 million were closely related to that of J Pierpoint Morgan.

Above: Mrs J B Ismay, who survived the disaster.

ways than in books. Already he had established for himself a considerable reputation as an antiquarian bibliophile with an especially well-chosen collection. In his memory his mother gave to Harvard University the great library which bears his name.

A familiar name on the passenger list was that of J Bruce Ismay. The son of T H Ismay, founder of White Star, J B Ismay had been educated at Harrow and privately in Dinard. An excellent sportsman, he had returned from a world tour to his father's shipping office to learn business. The story is told of his first day there: having deposited his hat and coat in his father's private room, the latter instructed a subordinate, in the hearing of the staff, to instruct the new office boy to leave his hat and coat somewhere else. Upon his father's death in 1899 Bruce Ismay inherited control of White Star. Reserved and retiring by nature, his was not the personality to see off the American financiers who took over the firm just three years later. He had attended the launch of the *Titanic* but was evidently not sufficiently interested in the mechanics of the great liner to join her for her sea trials. One suspects that Bruce Ismay was living in the shadow of other men, notably his father and Pirrie, when it came to the family business of shipbuilding. He was traveling with Thomas Andrews, manager of Harland and Wolff, on this maiden voyage, just as he had done a year previously on the *Olympic.*

Other passengers included Charles M Hays, Canadian president of Grand Trunk Pacific Railroad Companies, Clarence Moore, Master of the Chevy Chase Hunt, Clinch Smith, a well known man-about-town, Major Archibald Butt, military aide to President Taft and his friend Francis Millet, a well-known artist and author who was also an accomplished raconteur. Others aboard the *Titanic* counted among their professions merchants, stockbrokers, clergymen, lawyers, actors, gamblers, factory workers, and farm laborers many of whom had come from central Europe and Ireland. Indeed the passengers aboard the *Titanic* may fairly be said to represent a cross-section of society in the twilight years of what Mark Twain called a 'Gilded Age.'

The third wealthiest man aboard the *Titanic* was Isidor Straus who with his wife, Ida, was to become a principal hero of the tragedy. Unlike Astor or Guggenheim, Straus was a self-made man. He had settled in Georgia some time before the Civil War and as a salesman of Confederate bonds had acquired a reputation for exceptional probity. After branching out into glassware and china Isidor and his brother had leased a small corner of the recently established New York store R H Macy. After ten years they owned the store. Even though in recent years Isador had allowed the management of the store to devolve on his sons he was still worth at least $50 million.

A fourth name of note was that of Widener. The Wideners had made their fortune in the tramway business and at the time of their death Widener father and son were worth some $50 million. The son, who at the age of 27 was one of the youngest of the super rich to drown, was less interested in tram-

Above: Mr and Mrs George Harder; this photograph reminds us that the *Titanic* was a tragedy for ordinary folk, as well as for the rich and famous.

THE CREW

The crew on the *Titanic* numbered some 860 men of whom 340 worked below decks in the engine department as engineers, trimmers, boilermakers, greasemen, window cleaners, or linen keepers. Only a few dozen were actually engaged in seamanship directly and of these even fewer were officers.

The two points of contact between passengers and crew were to be found in the per-

Above: Captain E J Smith.

Left: The Officers of the *Titanic.* Standing, from left to right: Herbert McElroy, Chief Purser; Charles Lightoller, Second Officer; Herbert Pitman, Third Officer; Joseph Boxhall, Fourth Officer; Harold Lowe, Fifth Officer (all survived). Seated, from left to right: James Moody, Sixth Officer; Henry Wilde, Chief Officer; Captain Smith; William Murdoch, First Officer (all drowned).

Right: Chief Officer Wilde 'one of the bravest men who ever stepped on deck,' drowned when the ship sank.

Right: Fifth Officer Harold Lowe, one of the survivors among the crew.

Officer and Herbert Lightoller Second Officer. The other officer who regularly dined with the passengers was the Purser. Purser Hugh McElroy, approaching retirement age, seems to have been almost as popular as the Captain. His strong sense of humor was so popular with the passengers that they often timed their journeys to sail with him. Many a time he had held his own with a difficult passenger without giving cause for offense.

The three dozen or so other deck officers rarely came into direct contact with the passengers. Theirs was a working environment in which 'duty linked up with duty until the watches went by without pause or hitch.' The life of these officers centered around the bridge. On the after part of the bridge was the wheelhouse containing the wheel and steering compass and telephones leading to the crow's nest, engine room, poop, and fo'c'sle head. Also in the wheelhouse was the course-board on which the course would be chalked. Either side of the wheelhouse were the Captain's quarters and some of the Officers' rooms. It was from the bridge, situated some

sons of the Purser and the Captain. Captain E J Smith had started his apprenticeship in sailing ships before the Boer War and had risen through the ranks to become a Captain. By the time of the *Titanic*'s maiden voyage he had sailed some two million miles for White Star and they had complete confidence in him, entrusting to him the command of their best and newest liners. At £1250 a year his salary was the highest of any man afloat. With his uniform frock-coat, fluffy beard, and dignified bearing he looked the part and inspired confidence in his fellow officers and in his passengers. Then as now it was part of a Captain's duties to cultivate the grander passengers, and a seat at the Captain's table in the center of the huge dining room was much sought after. He enjoyed the confidence of bishops and millionaires alike and several of them had crossed the ocean with him many times before.

This was to be EJ's last voyage before his retirement and he seems to have taken special steps to ensure that it would be both safe and pleasurable. To this end he requested that his Chief Officer from the *Olympic*, Henry Wilde, be transferred to the same position on the *Titanic* for her maiden voyage. This meant that two *Titanic* officers had to move down a rung. W M Murdoch became First

Right: The deck of the *Olympic* is scrubbed. Note the lifeboat davits in the background.

190 feet from the bow, that Captain Smith, Cheif Officer Wilde, First Officer Murdoch and Second Officer Lightoller and their fellow officers worked four-hour shifts directing the activities on the rest of the ship which would enable it to achieve a safe and speedy passage.

In this they were assisted by other men with more specific functions. The *Titanic* carried six lookouts who, two at a time, scoured the horizon for two hours at a stretch. From their lofty perch in the crow's nest they would report anything unusual to the bridge. Other duties included those of the quartermaster. The quartermaster was stationed on the poop and it was his job to note the reading on the dial of the patent log fixed to the taffrail, telephone it to the bridge and enter it in his log book. The standby quartermaster had the job of running messages and other odd jobs such as reading the thermometer and the barometer, taking the temperature of the water, and reading the log. Every half hour he would sound the bell which was then acknowledged by the crow's nest.

A bell was also sounded at the end of each two-hour watch when a new helmsman would appear on the bridge to take the helm. At the same time a new Officer of the watch would come on duty and, after having ascertained the ship's position, course, and speed, examined the chart, checked the course being

Left: At 45,000 tons the Olympic-class vessels were the largest steamers in existence.

steered, learned from his predecessor all the 'items of interest' such as weather conditions, wireless messages and so on and, having accustomed his eyes to the darkness if it was night, he would officially 'take over' the watch. He was now responsible for everything that occurred during the watch and in this he was assisted by his junior officers.

At noon all the officers would gather together with their sextants to make a dead reckoning of their position. This was particularly important when steering a Great Circle course since this necessitated frequent alterations of course. Solar and stellar bearings were taken frequently to check the compass error inherent in steering such a course.

We have now met the passengers and been introduced to the officers and their equipment which were to have brought the pride of the White Star Company safely from the Old World to the New on this her maiden voyage. It is time to begin that journey.

THE TITANIC MAKES READY

Above: Lord Pirrie (left), Chairman of Harland and Wolff, and (right) J Bruce Ismay, Chairman of White Star, inspect the *Titanic*.

AFTER a number of delays which resulted from several mishaps which befell her sister-ship, the *Titanic* underwent a brief series of sea trials in Belfast Lough and was deemed fit for passenger service. She left Belfast in time to reach Ocean Dock in Southampton by 3 April. There she would be laden with provisions and furnished with a crew. White Star's newest ship was received with much excitement by the people of Southampton who, to this day, regard her as a Southampton ship.

Britain was in the grip of a coal strike which meant that at least two other IMM ships, the *Oceanic* and the *Adriatic*, were raided for the precious fuel which would enable the *Titanic* to depart on schedule for her maiden voyage. Crew members were also transferred from other ships for the same purpose. Meanwhile the formidable task of loading supplies continued. A glance at the list of on-board provisions drawn up by her chief chef gives us some idea of the scale of the operation. On his list we find that he required, for example, 75,000 pounds of fresh meat, 35,000 fresh eggs, 40 tons of potatoes, 800 bundles of asparagus, 1000 bottles of wine, and 15,000 bottles of ale and stout. Other requirements were 12,000 dinner plates, 1,000 oyster forks, 15,000 champagne glasses, 40,000 towels of different sorts and

Launch
OF
White Star Royal Mail Triple-Screw Steamer

"TITANIC"

At BELFAST,

Wednesday, 31st May, 1911, at 12·15 p.m.

Admit Bearer.

Left: Invitation to the launch of the *Titanic*, 31 May 1911.

Above: Spectators watch from the great gantry as the *Titanic* is launched.

Right: The *Titanic* in Belfast Lough.

Above: The *Titanic* during fitting out. Note the specially constructed floating crane.

Right: The *Titanic* in harbor at Southampton, England.

45,000 table napkins. It took the experienced dockers of Southampton less than a week to load the ship and make her ready for her maiden voyage scheduled for 10 April 1912.

THE PASSENGERS ASSEMBLE

Southampton was enjoying a bright rather fresh April day when the 9.45 Waterloo Boat Train entered the port area. As the train drew up beside the platform running parallel with the newly extended White Star quay, the name *Titanic* was on everyone's lips; the passengers gazed 75 feet up at the enormous hull which completely dwarfed all other shipping in the port. Three plumes of smoke emerged from her funnels. The Blue Peter flew at her fore yardarm while at her mainmast flew the house flag of the White Star Line and at her foremast the Stars and Stripes. The seven letters TITANIC were inscribed in gold on her bows. All agreed that she was an extremely handsome ship with a sleek and simple design which belied her size. She had not that heaviness of appearance which characterized other large liners of her day. She represented Harland and Wolff's design philosophies perfectly and the yard manager, Thomas Andrews, was there to enjoy her. So too was J B Ismay who had motored down from London with his family the previous day.

At noon, when the boat train arrived, the great ship was already swarming with people – members of the crew, shore officials, tradesmen, contractors, inspectors, messengers, visitors of all kinds, and the friends of the passengers besides a large number of passengers themselves. The Purser Hugh McElroy and his two assistants were at their busiest. For their part the surgeons were swiftly and expertly examining each steerage passenger for traces of trachoma. Once past the surgeons a team of stewards efficiently led them to their accommodations.

SHE'S OFF

Soon after noon, the *Titanic*'s huge siren boomed out and those not making the crossing were escorted off the ship. The gangways were lowered and the tugs made fast. With a distant tremor the engines began to turn as inch by inch the gap between the black hull and the quay widened. With handkerchiefs waving the crowds raised a cheer: 'She's off.' Very slowly the greatest liner in the world

glided away from the quay and with her escort of tugs crept toward the entrance of the dock.

It was at this moment that disaster nearly struck. The displacement of such a large volume of water in an enclosed space, combined with the effect of an offshore breeze, caused a moored liner, the *New York*, to snap her moorings. As tug boats frantically attempted to get a line on the American liner Captain Smith first cut his engines, and then deftly used the wash from his port engine to halt the swing of the other ship. The *New York*'s stern cleared the *Titanic*'s port quarter by a matter of inches.

The incident was regarded with not a little misgiving by certain passengers. Thus it was that Mrs Harris, wife of an American impresario, found herself suddenly addressed by a stranger: 'This is a bad omen,' he told her, adding 'Do you love life?' She replied simply, 'I love it.' 'Then get off this ship at Cher-

Below: The *Titanic* leaves Southampton at 1.00 pm, 10 April 1912. Note the Flying Bridge and Crow's Nest.

bourg . . . That's what I'm going to do.'

E J Smith maneuvered his huge ship through Southampton Water, round Calshot Spit, and through the narrow Thorn Channel with consummate skill. After rounding the hazardous West Bramble the ship gathered speed as it steamed past the green lawns and leveled telescopes of the Royal Yacht Squadron at West Cowes. It was here that the beauty and symmetry of her lines could be seen to best advantage.

Now that the intricate s-shaped channel out of Southampton was safely astern and the pilot dropped off, Captain Smith could order 'full speed ahead.' While the passengers set about finding their way around the ship and had their tea the *Titanic* proceeded toward the French coast at Cherbourg. En route it was discovered that the binoculars which were normally provided for the lookouts were missing. This fact was communicated to the First Officer who replied that there were none. It seems that a pair had been provided – as on the *Oceanic* – but they had gone missing as part of the reshuffle of senior officers at Southampton. As the sun sank toward the western horizon the coast of France came into sight. The *Titanic* lay that evening in the Cherbourg Roads. It was here that she picked up passengers who were returning from their winter sojourns in the fashionable resorts in the South of France. They had with them their own personal maids and valets as well as a staggering quantity of luggage. Mrs Charlotte Drake Cardeza, for example, had with her no less than fourteen trunks, four suit-

Below: The graceful profile of the *Titanic*.

Right and below right: The popularity of the great White Star liners is reflected in the number of popular postcards produced at the time.

Below: The *Olympic* in New York harbor.

WHITE STAR LINE.

TRIPLE-SCREW R.M.S. "OLYMPIC," 46,439 TONS, THE LARGEST BRITISH STEAMER, AT NEW YORK.

funnels (presumably the dummy one used for ventilation). An American lady later attributed the loss of the *Titanic* to this apparition. It was here also that a young fireman, John Coffey, was struck with sudden foreboding and deserted his ship. They were not the only people to feel uneasy. For no less a person than the Chief Officer that day was saying of the ship that 'I have a queer feeling about it.'

Soon the *Titanic*'s siren sounded, the tenders cast off, and the bum boats stood clear. The huge anchor was raised and the great screws began to revolve as she headed westward once more, the tapering spire of St Colman's Cathedral disappearing into the distance. As she cruised 45 miles off the southern Irish coast, the lookouts once again

Above: When transatlantic travel cost less than £15.

Below: Information for passengers aboard White Star Line ships.

cases, and three crates of baggage. With all the new passengers aboard, the *Titanic* set sail for Queenstown, Ireland.

Passengers and crew settled into the routines of life on the *Titanic*. It was on this leg of the journey that Captain Smith sent the ship through an s-shaped maneuver presumably so that he could get the mettle of his new command.

It was not until late in the forenoon of Thursday 11 April that the distant gray mountains of Cork rose slowly from the sea. Taking on board a pilot, the *Titanic* steamed slowly through the Heads, rounded Roches Point and finally anchored 2 miles out to sea. The 150 or so passengers who embarked at Queenstown were mostly steerage class: they trooped aboard in small parties of relatives and friends – Dalys, Flynns, Kellys, McCoys, Murphys, O'Briens, O'Connors, and Ryans. It was here that a strange incident took place; as one of the tenders was coming alongside some of the passengers saw a soot-covered fireman's face appear from one of the

INFORMATION FOR PASSENGERS.

BREAKFAST from 8 until 10 o'clock.

LUNCHEON at 1 p.m.   *DINNER* at 7 o'clock.

The Bar opens at 8 a.m., and closes at 11·30 p.m.

Lights are extinguished in the Saloon at 11 p.m., Lounge at 11·30 p.m., and Smoke Room at 12 Midnight.

DIVINE SERVICE in the Saloon on Sunday at 10·30 a.m.

SEATS AT TABLE. Passengers who have not previously arranged for seats at table to be reserved should apply for same to the Second Steward.

Children are not entitled to seats in the Saloon unless full fare is paid.

WIRELESS TELEGRAMS. All Southampton — Cherbourg — Queenstown — New York, Liverpool—Queenstown—New York, Liverpool—Quebec—Montreal, Liverpool—Halifax—Portland, and Liverpool—Queenstown—Boston Mail and Passenger Steamers of the White Star Line are fitted with the Marconi system of Wireless Telegraphy, and messages for despatch should be handed in at the Enquiry Office.

AN ENQUIRY OFFICE has been provided for the convenience of Passengers, where all enquiries for information of a general character should be made.

Letters, Cables, Telegrams and Marconigrams are received here for despatch, and Postage Stamps can be purchased, and Deck Chairs and Steamer Rugs hired at this office, through which also all Mails will be distributed.

None of the ship's staff other than those on duty in the Enquiry Office are authorised to accept Letters or Telegrams for despatch.

CABLEGRAMS and **TELEGRAMS** should be handed in at the Enquiry Office an hour before the arrival at any port called at.

THE SURGEON is authorised to make customary charges, subject in each case to the approval of the Commander, for treating passengers at their request for any illness not originating on board the ship. In the case of sickness developed on board no charge will be made, and medicine will be provided free in all circumstances.

BAGGAGE. Questions relating to Baggage should be referred to the Second Steward, who is the Ship's Baggage Master. Trunks, Chairs which Passengers may desire to leave in charge of the Company, should be properly labelled and handed to the Baggage Master on the Wharf at New York, and such articles will be stored entirely at owner's risk. It is necessary for passengers themselves to see all their Baggage is passed by the U.S. Customs Authorities on landing.

DECK CHAIRS can be hired at a charge of 4/- each for the voyage.

STEAMER RUGS can be hired at a charge of 4/- each for the voyage.

PASSENGERS are requested to ask for a Receipt on the Company's Form, for any additional Passage Money, Chair or Steamer Rug Hire, or Freight paid on board.

EXCHANGE OF MONEY. The Purser is prepared, for the convenience of passengers, to exchange a limited amount of English and American money, and he will allow at the rate of $4·80 to the £1 when giving American money for English currency, or £1 for $4·95 when giving English money for American money.

The following rates of exchange have also been adopted for American and French and German money—Eastbound, $1 = 5 Francs = 4 Marks; Westbound, Notes and Gold—19 cents per Franc or 23 cents per Mark; Silver—18 cents per Franc or 22 cents per Mark.

repeated their request for the binoculars. About teatime the circular tower of the Fastnet light was sighted but by the time that the bugle was sounded for dinner the coast had disappeared into the darkness.

The *Titanic* followed the standard outward-bound track for mail steamers to the Nantucket light vessel off Massachusetts. This was the Great Circle course from the Fastnet rock to what was known as 'the Corner' which was situated off the coast of Cape Race in the vicinity of latitude 42° North and longitude 47° West. From there she was to have proceeded by rhumb line to Sandy Hook.

The *Titanic* was well out in the Atlantic by daybreak on the 12th and that day and the following days were spent enjoying the facilities on board. As Dr Washington Dodge observed 'The weather was fine and calm. At all times one might walk the deck with the same security as if walking down the market street, so little motion was there to the vessel. It was hard to realise that one was not in some large and sumptuous hotel.'

The evenings were spent dining and listening to the ship's orchestra who played a medley of extracts from operetta, music hall and popular melodies under the leadership of Wallace Hartley. As well as these old favorites Hartley had brought with him some of the latest music such as 'The Bunny Hug' and 'The Turkey Trot.' The orchestra performed each day to a large number of people in various parts of the vessel and contributed greatly to the gaiety which prevailed on board the *Titanic*. Mrs René Harris summed up the atmosphere many years later: 'We were out on a lark and revelry was the keynote. The days passed too quickly. I felt as if I would like to go on until the end of time. Dinner parties, bridge parties, dancing, auction pools, and midnight repasts were indulged in to the nth degree.'

Passengers kept in touch with the outside world by reading the *Atlantic Daily Bulletin*. This comprised a dozen or so pre-printed pages of articles of a literary, artistic, or scientific nature to which were added the news items of the day as picked up by the two Marconi operators. Of special interest to the first-class passengers aboard the *Titanic* was the in-

R·M·S· TITANIC·

formation regarding the booming London Stock Exchange.

As the *Titanic* continued her westward voyage Captain Smith gradually increased her speed. On the first day out she had covered 386 miles. On the second the figure rose to 519 and on the third to 546 miles. White Star prided itself on sticking to its schedules since, as Mrs Douglas observed, 'all were interested in getting into New York early.' By the time the passengers heard the bugle for breakfast on the morning of Sunday 14 April, more boilers had been lit and the speed increased from 21 to about 22½ knots.

Above: A contemporary postcard of the *Titanic* showing its wireless aerials.

SUNDAY 14 APRIL

Above: The finest vessel in the world.

SUNDAY 14th was a fine day, with a smooth sea and moderate south-westerly wind. Strolling on the sheltered promenade decks 70 feet above the water, the first-class passengers could see the Atlantic sparkling in the sunshine as it stretched away to the far horizon. For the crew, though, Sunday was not a day for relaxation. It was the day of the Captain's inspection and everything about the vessel had to be shipshape. Every part of the ship was visited by the Captain, the Chief Officer, the Chief Engineer, the Purser and the Chief Surgeon, who proceeded, with measured tread, in full uniform from stem to stern and from the topmost to the lowest deck. Sunday was also the usual day for boat drill on the White Star line, but for some reason this drill was done away with on this particular Sunday.

At eleven o'clock Captain Smith conducted a church service using the company's special prayer book. This lasted about forty minutes and was followed by lunch. Over lunch the Assistant Purser had told certain passengers that despite the previous day's improved run of 546 miles, they would still not be able to arrive in New York until Wednesday morning and not Tuesday night as had previously been expected. It was also at lunch that two clergymen on board had asked the Assistant Bursar whether they might use the dining room that night for a service of hymns. One of these clergymen, Beesley, then retired to the library to read. Later in life he would recall that sunny Sunday afternoon spent in the peace and quiet of the wide and airy library aboard the *Titanic*.

Elsewhere in the ship things were not so serene. Deep in the stokehold the 'blackgang' stripped to the waist were busy shooting load after load of coal against the blazing furnaces which provided the steam to drive the huge

Right: Passengers enjoying a stroll on the boat deck.

Left: The William-and-Mary style grand stairway formed a focal point for the first-class passengers.

The grand stairway and reception room adjoining the restaurant.

propellors. 24 out of the total of 29 boilers were lit by this stage of the voyage and the heat in the stokehold was terrific. Elsewhere the Marconi operators, Senior Operator Jack Phillips and his Junior, Harold Bride, were also hard at work. Late on Friday they had discovered a fault with the transmitter. Much of Saturday had been spent repairing this and a backlog of telegrams had developed. Despite this breakdown, Phillips and Bride had still managed to send off some 250 marconigrams since the departure from Southampton. Both operators, however, were extremely tired by this stage in the voyage and it was for this reason that Bride had undertaken to relieve Phillips on Sunday night at midnight instead of at the usual time of 2 am. That night the Wideners and a number of friends had enjoyed the Captain's company at dinner. After dinner he lingered over a cigar, enjoying no doubt the atmosphere and suc-

cess of this his last cruise, before returning to the bridge just before nine o'clock.

Up on the bridge Captain Smith commented to Second Officer Lightoller that it was a cold and windless night. Lightoller agreed, adding that it was a pity that the breeze had not kept up. After a brief tour of the bridge Captain Smith retired. As he left he told his Second Officer that if it became in the slightest degree hazy they would have to slow down: 'if it becomes at all doubtful let me know at once; I will be just inside.' This was the customary reminder of a Captain retiring for the night.

The reason why the two officers had hoped for a breeze on this clear but cold night was that there had been a number of reports of ice in the region that they were approaching. In a 'flat calm' the lookouts with or without binoculars could not expect to detect an iceberg on the horizon since this was done by

looking out for ripples breaking at the base of the iceberg.

Ice reports had been received by the *Titanic*'s radio operators from as early in the voyage as Friday 12th, when the French liner *Touraine* had dispatched an ice warning to the *Titanic* at about 7 pm. On Sunday 14th the ice reports became more frequent. Shortly before 1 pm the *Baltic* sent the following message:

Captain, *Titanic* – Have had moderate, variable winds and clear, fine weather since leaving. Greek steamer *Athenai* reports passing icebergs and large quantities of field ice today in latitude 41° 51′ North, longitidute 49° 52′ West. . . . Wish you and *Titanic* all success. Commander.

This and the previous messages were formally acknowledged by the Master. Later Captain Smith handed J B Ismay the *Baltic*'s marconigram without comment, as Ismay talked to passengers before going in to luncheon. It seems that the message lay in Ismay's pocket until shortly before dinner time. Certainly the officers on duty had no knowledge of it. That same afternoon mes-

Above: Passengers on the spacious deck.

Below: The gym with rowing machine, electric camel etc.

sages from the *Amerika* and the *Antillian* were picked up which now referred directly to icebergs rather than field ice.

During the afternoon of Sunday 14 April the *Titanic* reached the 'Corner' or turning point. Here it was usual for vessels following the Great Circle to change course in the direction of Sandy Hook. It was with some surpise then that the Fourth Officer found that the course had not already been altered when he came on duty in the first dog watch (4-6 pm). It seems likely that Captain Smith was, by continuing on his course, endeavoring to steer clear of some of the ice which had been reported. For the *Titanic* had already received at least seven ice warnings that Sunday and it was the general opinion of the officers that she would be 'up with the ice' at some time between 10 pm and midnight.

Certainly the watchkeepers on duty from about 6 pm were looking out for it. At 7.15 Murdoch had said to a lamp trimmer, 'Hemming, when you go forward get the fire scuttle hatch closed. There is a glow left from that, and as we are in the vicinity of ice I want everything dark before the bridge.'

At about 9.45 pm, soon after the Captain had left the bridge, Lightoller told the Sixth Officer to warn the men in the crow's nest of the need to keep an especially sharp look out for ice until daybreak, particularly small ice and growlers (icebergs less than 15 feet tall

and 50 feet long). After acknowledging the order Jewell turned to his mate Symons and murmured: 'It is very cold here.' Symons replied, 'Yes; by the smell of it there is ice about.'

At 10 pm when First Officer Murdoch relieved Lightoller the two discussed the weather, mentioning as they did so the lack of definition between the horizon and the sky. This would make an iceberg all the more difficult to see on a calm night, especially if it had a black side which was turned their way. However, both agreed that except for this it was an extremely clear night. What neither man knew as they changed watch was that about half an hour earlier a message had been received warning the *Titanic* of an immense mass of ice lying dead in her track:

Below: In spite of the tragedy of the *Titanic,* White Star went on to launch her second sister-ship, the *Britannic.*

From *Mesaba* to *Titanic* . . . the report in latitude 42° North to 41° 25', longitude 49° to 50° 30' West. Saw much heavy pack ice and a great number large icebergs. Also field ice. Weather good, clear.

The *Titanic* answered 'Received; thanks.'

Such a message would normally be delivered to the Master of a vessel and acknowledged by him. S H Adams, the *Mesaba*'s operator, waited for that acknowledgment in vain, as he heard the *Titanic* once again continue with its calls to Cape Race. There seems to be no good reason why Marconi-operator Phillips should have left the message under a paperweight and, by so doing, disregarded the regulation that priority should always be given to messages affecting the navigation of the vessel. An hour and 20 minutes later, Phillips deliberately disregarded that regulation when he told a Leyland liner, the S S *Californian*, to stop jamming his signals to M C E at Cape Race: 'Shut up. Shut up. I am busy working Cape Race.'

Evans, the operator on the *Californian* was inexperienced and did not persist. The *Californian* had been brought to a halt in an ice flow and was apparently attempting to warn

ROYAL AND UNITED STATES Mail Steamer

"BRITANNIC"

(TRIPLE SCREW)

LAUNCHED AT BELFAST
26th February 1914.

WHITE STAR LINE
"OLYMPIC" 45,324 TONS
Verdens største Dampskibe

BRITANNIC

"White Star" Royal Mail Steamer "Olympic"
Tonnage 45,000 tons, Length 882½ feet,
Breadth 92½ feet.

These pages: This selection of contemporary postcards of the *Olympic* and *Britannic* reveals the extent to which the great liners had entered the popular imagination – even (top left) in Denmark!

43

Above: The mail room on F deck. 3420 sacks of mail went down with the ship.

Far right: A cross-section of the ship showing the double bottom.

Below: a fanciful drawing of the *Titanic* being struck by ice.

the *Titanic* of the proximity of ice. Phillips had disregarded the regulations in failing to inform the bridge of these ice warnings, coming as they did after four previous warnings (from the *Caronia, Baltic, Amerika,* and *Antillian*). However at 10.30 pm the Officers of the Watch on the *Titanic* had been informed directly of the approach of dangerous ice. The Master of the *Rappahannoch* which was steaming on an opposite course to the *Titanic* passed the following message to her by signal lamp: 'Have just passed through heavy ice field and several icebergs.'

The *Titanic* simply acknowledged him:

'Message received. Thanks. Good night' and continued to steam into the night. If one plotted the position of the vessels which warned the *Titanic* of ice on Sunday 14 April on a chart they would form a parallelogram. It was into the midst of the area represented by that parallelogram that her experienced First Officer was now navigating, and that at a speed of 22½ knots on an oily sea. The reasons why Murdoch did not awaken Captain Smith are unclear. Presumably he trusted the lookouts to spot an iceberg in sufficient time for him to be able to take avoiding action. The questions must be raised of how far and how clearly could the lookouts see an approaching iceberg. To do this we must climb up to the crow's nest.

At the same time as Murdoch relieved Lightoller on the bridge, lookouts Fleet and Lee had climbed the ladder inside the forward mast and positioned themselves in the crow's nest, Lee on the starboard side and Fleet on the port. Visibility from the bridge was particularly good, even though there was no moon – indeed Murdoch could even see the stars 'heading down towards the horizon.' However, this would not necessarily have been the case in the crow's nest; as Fleet and Lee continued to gaze intently at the horizon from their positions in the crow's nest, it seems that a haze began to develop and thicken. No record, though, exists of the lookouts having reported any visibility problems to the bridge as the *Titanic* steamed into the night.

THE IMPACT

The lookouts were freezing cold and looking forward to returning to the warmth of the ship. Then with only 20 minutes to go Fleet half saw an object in the hazy darkness ahead of him. Seconds later he struck three bells and reached across for the telephone: 'Iceberg right ahead' he informed Sixth Officer Moody. The Sixth Officer said thank you and informed Murdoch.

Immediately the First Officer ordered 'Hard-a-starboard' (ie that the ship should go to port). He then telegraphed the engine room 'Stop. Full speed astern.' He pulled the switch that closed the watertight doors in the

boiler and engine rooms and waited anxiously as the ship's head veered slowly to port. But no sooner was the helm hard over than they all felt a jolt, followed by a grinding noise far below them on the starboard side. Captain Smith rushed out of his quarters:

'Mr Murdoch, what was that?'

'An iceberg sir. I hard-a-starboarded and reversed engines and I was going to hard-a-port round it but she was too close. I could not do any more. I have closed the watertight doors.'

AFTER THE COLLISION

The *Titanic* had not struck the iceberg head-on but rather had glanced past it. As the 46,000-ton ship slowly lost headway, the officers on the bridge could see astern 'a small black mass not rising very high out of the water.' The first task for the Captain was to assess the damage to his ship.

Boxhall was dispatched to make a quick examination of the damage. But despite descending to the lowest steerage quarters beneath the foc's'le head he could find no damage. Soon, however, the ship's carpenter arrived on the bridge to announce that 'the ship is making water.' He was closely followed by a mail clerk who told the Captain that the mail hold was filling rapidly. By the time that the Chief Officer had arrived, the true seriousness of the situation was becoming apparent. Already the commutator showed a list to starboard of 5 degrees. As the water entered the gash created by the iceberg Murdoch enquired of the Captain whether the situation was serious.

'I'm afraid it's more than serious,' was the response. The man who knew most about the design of the ship was T H Andrews of Harland and Wolff. He was hastily called to the bridge. The Captain and Andrews then descended below the waterline. They found that the sea was entering six forward compartments. Despite the employment of powerful pumps, water was continuing to rise in these compartments and since they only extended as far as F and E decks it was clear to both of them that, as each compartment was flooded, so the water would pour

into the next and so on until all 16 compartments had been flooded. Andrews' expert prognosis was that the ship had an hour or an hour and a half to live.

Soon Captain Smith ordered the Chief Officer to have the covers stripped off the lifeboats and the Bo'sun piped 'all hands on deck.' In fact this last command was somewhat superfluous since by this stage the crew had been awakened by the sound of steam escaping, 'kicking up a row that would have dwarfed the row of a thousand railway engines thundering through a culvert.' The sound was coming from the ship's eight exhausts. In the face of such a deafening shriek, communication on deck was extremely diffi-

Below: The *Olympic* in Plymouth harbor dwarfs other ships and boats.

Right: T H Andrews of Harland and Wolff. After the *Titanic* struck ice he gave her an hour and a half to live. Although the ship stayed afloat for an hour longer than that, Andrews was among those lost.

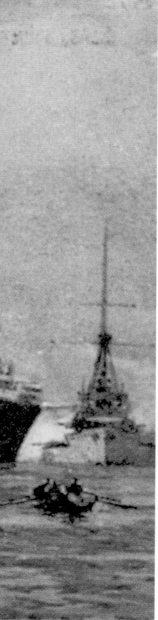

MGY, and the vesssel's approximate position of 41° 44′ North, 50° 24′ West. Some ten minutes later the Captain reappeared in the wireless room and enquired of the operators, 'What are you sending?'

'CQD' replied Phillips.

Bride suggested that they should send SOS instead since 'it's the new call and it may be your last chance to send it.' At this the three of them laughed. The new message was CQD CQD SOS SOS CQD. This message was picked up by two vessels, the *Frankfurt* and the *Carpathia*. Their respective masters were sent for and another message sent by the *Titanic*.

CQD CQD SOS SOS CQD SOS. Come at once. We have struck a berg. CQD [ie. it's a CQD, old man]. Position 41° 46′ North, 50° 14′ West CQD SOS.

This more detailed message contained the revised position as calculated by Boxhall and would enable the ships in the vicinity to come to her aid more speedily. In all at least five ships picked up the distress calls, including her White Star sister ship, the *Olympic* which was steaming eastwards but at too great a distance to be of direct help in a rescue. The 13,564-ton Cunard liner *Carpathia* was, however, much closer and all rivalries between the two companies were automatically put aside. On reading the *Titanic*'s message her Master, Arthur Rostron, immediately ordered an about-turn and headed his ship at full speed towards the *Titanic*'s position

cult. This and the fact that the lifeboat crews had, apparently, received no training, hampered their progress. Fourth Officer Boxhall supervised the stripping of the boats, but soon he was needed on the bridge. The captain ordered Boxhall to make a calculation of the ship's position – based on the stellar observations of 7.30 pm. His calculated position was then taken to the wireless room to be used in the distress signals.

Captain Smith personally asked the two wireless operators to send out a call for assistance at 12.15 am, half an hour after the initial impact. The call used was the 'Regular International General Distress Call': CQD six times, followed by the *Titanic*'s call sign,

employing no less than 14 lookouts for the purpose.

Phillips despatched Bride to the bridge to inform Captain Smith of the good news. During the next hour or so Bride made repeated trips to the bridge with news of the *Carpathia*'s progress toward the stricken vessel. In some ways therefore he was among the best informed men aboard the *Titanic*. Elsewhere anything from chaos, incomprehension, and confusion to a total indifference governed the emotions of the passengers and crew after the impact.

It was in the foc's'le and steerage quarters that the nature of the collision was first brought home. The grinding crash had alarmed or awakened many members of the crew and passengers in these quarters. Further sounds which caused alarm were the telegraph bell of the engine room, the sudden reversal of the engines and the ringing of the bells that warned of the imminent closure of the watertight bulkhead doors. The passengers in the third class were awakened less by the sound of the impact than by the sight and sound of water swirling about the deck. Many of them dressed and crowded into the corridors where they bumped into members of the crew who were already heading for their boat stations.

The passengers in the first class were those most cushioned from the sights and sounds of the collision and even some time after the impact most were unaware that their floating hotel had been delivered of a death wound. Most of those who had gone to bed after dinner carried on sleeping while even those who were awake seem to have been little concerned by the slight jar which had been felt. Thus a cotton broker from Philadelphia con-

Below: A Renaissance stateroom on the 'floating hotel.'

Left: The card room
aboard the *Homeric*.

Right: the smoking
room aboard the
Olympic combined 'the
dignity of a club with
the intimate comfort of
a room at home.'

tinued to dictate a letter at a time when, in the depths of the ship, the boilermen were already waist-high in freezing cold water. Even on the few occasions when the passengers had come out of their rooms to see what had happened they were apparently told by a steward that it was nothing serious, but that they would be delayed for two hours.

The accounts of Martha Eustis Stevenson and Elizabeth Eustis are typical of many. For although they had heard the impact, indeed had been alarmed by it, they had at no point been awoken by a member of crew. Instead their friend John Thayer had found them in their room:

He was very glad that we had dressed. He thought there was no danger, but we had struck ice and there was much on deck and he urged us to come up and see it.

Once on the deck they encountered a steward who called out, 'All back to the state rooms for life preservers.' Only then did the seriousness of the situation begin to dawn on them.

One of the most level-headed accounts of the tragedy was that told by the young schoolmaster Lawrence Beesley. He was a second-class passenger who had felt 'nothing more than an extra heave of the engines' during the collision. He had gone up on deck to find out why the ship's engines had stopped, wrongly concluding that she must have dropped a propellor blade. Finding the deck deserted he entered the smoking room where a game of cards was in mid flow. Here he was informed that the occupants of the smoking room had recently seen an iceberg go by which towered above the decks. None of those present though had been sufficiently interested in this spectacle to go out on deck to take a clear look.

At this stage no official call had gone out from the bridge for a general muster on the boat decks and although, in certain quarters, people were being urged to put on lifebelts, in other areas crowds were still smoking and playing cards. Gradually, however, crowds began to gather in the lounges, foyers, and on the boat deck. As they did so, McElroy found the Purser's office besieged by a crowd clamoring for their valuables. Only at 12.30 am, some three-quarters of an hour after the collision, did all the stateroom stewards come on

duty. Their job was to knock on the doors of all the cabins, to rouse the passengers, and get them to put on their lifebelts and warm clothing to combat the icy conditions.

Even in the first class a sense of urgency had entered the situation as they were ushered up to the boat deck. That the ship was in distress should have been clear to everyone on board (according to Beesley). For Captain Smith had authorized the sending up of distress rockets 'whose flash illumined at the same time the faces and minds of the obedient crowd, the one with mere physical light, the other with a sudden revelation of what its message was. Everyone knew . . . we were calling for help from anyone near enough to see.' Specifically, the rockets were aimed at attracting the attention of a vessel (possibly the *Californian*) whose lights had been observed about 5 degrees on the port bow. The firing of the white rockets (eight in all) was interspersed with intense activity on the Morse lamp and in the Marconi room, but to no avail.

Below: The passengers' friends, Chief Purser McElroy and Captain Smith.

THE EVACUATION

Above: Captain Smith who inspired confidence in passengers and crew alike.

CAPTAIN Smith had been made aware of the seriousness of the situation soon after the collision. However, he failed to inform those supervising the loading of the lifeboats that he had sent out an international distress call and that the ship was sinking. Lightoller, the officer in charge of the lifeboats, only realized that the ship was actually doomed when he made his own inspection of a long narrow stairway which extended four decks below. It was his observation that water was creeping further up this stairway that eventually brought home to him the urgency of the situation. And by that stage he had already lowered four or five partially filled boats into the sea. For, as he said at the enquiry, he felt keenly the 'unutterable disgrace of going down with boats still hanging on the davits.'

There seems to have been no definite procedure either for the order or for the manner of the evacuation. When questioned at the American inquiry into the disaster, Lightoller explained that he had simply been following 'the rule of human nature' in evacuating the women and children first. As to the reason why the lifeboats were lowered only partially full, it seems there were a number of answers. It would appear that Second Officer Lightoller and Fifth Officer Lowe on the port

Below: One of the half-filled lifeboats.

and starboard sides respectively had lowered the boats half-full in the mistaken belief that they would have buckled in the middle if filled to capacity. It had been their intention to lower the boats to water level and then direct them to an open hatch at the bottom of a gangway so that they could fill up with more passengers. What Lightoller and Lowe did not notice was that the hatches almost 70 feet below them had long ago been covered by the rising sea water in the bottom of the ship. One of many questions never satisfactorily explained was why none of the experts from Harland and Wolff, or indeed the Captain himself, chose to inform Lightoller and Lowe of the possibility of filling the lifeboats to capacity at deck level.

The *Titanic* was equipped with 16 lifeboats and 4 emergency rafts; enough for some 1200 people. On the night of 14 April, however, only 700 people boarded the lifeboats. There was plenty of time and the weather conditions were perfect. What was worse was the fact that of those 700 many were crew and not passengers. Few of the crew on the *Titanic* were seasoned seamen with a knowledge of how to lower a lifeboat, and many of those who were had been put into the first lifeboats to accompany the women and children.

A rumor had spread around the *Titanic* that she would shortly be surrounded by rescue ships. This may account for the fact that the officer supervising the loading into the lifeboats frequently found it difficult to find enough takers to fill up the boats. There was ample room for all first- and second-class women and children in the boats, but it was only with difficulty that they could be persuaded to leave the light of the 'unsinkable ship' and make the perilous descent into the dark sea. The list of the boat to starboard meant that a gap nearly two and a half feet wide had formed between the lifeboats dangling over the ship's side and the deck. In some cases deckchairs were lashed together

Right: The lifeboats; there were too few of them and the crew was unfamiliar with the means of lowering them.

Left: The human drama of the evacuation.

to form a bridge, but later passengers had to jump across the gap. Lightoller positioned himself in the dangling lifeboats and caught the children thrown to him.

Many women would not be parted from their loved ones. Thus a couple of seamen were needed to drag Mrs Collyer from her husband who shouted 'Go Lottie. For God's sake, be brave and go! I'll get a seat in another boat.'

One woman who would not be parted from her husband was Mrs Straus. She

Above: A lifeboat dangles precariously as passengers scramble aboard.

Right: Lady Duff Gordon who escaped in a boat with 11 others.

simply threw her arms around her husband, declaring 'We are old people, Isidor, and we will die together.'

On the port side the rule of 'women and children only' had been rigidly enforced, but on the starboard, men were let through the ring of crewmen surrounding the boat, and there were many empty spaces. Thus it was that Lawrence Beesley was doubly lucky to escape that night. He was standing on the port side when he heard the call, 'Any more ladies?' He wrote the story himself:

'Looking over the side of the ship I saw boat # 13 swinging level with A Deck. It was half full of women. Again the call was repeated. 'Any more ladies?' I saw none coming. Then one of the crew looked up and said 'Any ladies on your deck, sir?' 'No,' I replied. 'Then you'd better jump,' said he. I dropped and fell into the bottom of the boat as they cried, 'Lower away.'

Beesley had waited patiently and seized his chance. A few others appear to have been downright selfish – though they defended themselves with spirit at the inquiries. It seems that Sir Cosmo and Lady Duff Gordon all but commandeered # 1 lifeboat for themselves and Lady Duff's secretary. Their boat left with only twelve on board and was, therefore, the worst example of underfilling that evening. Other tales make rather more edifying reading.

One such case was that of one of the youngest officers. James Moody stayed on board the *Titanic* long after he should have joined the other junior officers in rowing the liferafts. By staying with Chief Officer Wilde and First Officer Lightoller right to the end he was instrumental in saving many a life which might otherwise have been lost in the evacuation.

One of the things that was remarkable about the evacuation was the length of time that order was preserved. Some years later Lightoller wrote that 'the cool, calm unselfish courage exemplified throughout has never been excelled.' In writing this he was thinking not just of his Chief Officer who was 'one of the bravest men who ever stepped on deck' but of certain seamen and passengers as well. On one occasion for example Lightoller was left with only one man left to attend the boat falls for lowering away. 'Someone for that after fall' he called out, whereupon junior officer James Moody, whom he had ordered to take charge of the lifeboat responded 'Aye aye Sir' and stepped back on board the sinking *Titanic*. The members of the ship's orchestra also stayed at their posts well beyond the call of duty. Indeed one of the abiding myths surrounding the disaster is the image of the orchestra playing 'Nearer my God to Thee' as the ship went down. In fact it seems much more likely that they were playing rather more cheerful music. They had taken up position near the entrance to the first-class lounge at 12.15 am and ended up on the boat deck. From their changing position they had successfully raised the spirits of the passengers by regaling them with a stream of sprightly popular songs, rags, and waltzes. Shortly before the end they played the final hymn tune, *Autumn*.

Also worthy of especial mention was the behavior of Phillips and Bride, the Marconi operators. In the two hours after the collision with the iceberg they had kept up a steady transmission rate of 15 words a minute as they tried desperately to summon help from other ships. As Phillips continued to tap away Bride strapped a life belt to his back. Soon after they had sent the message 'Come quick. Our engine room flooded up to the boilers,' Captain Smith appeared once more

with the words: 'Men, you have done your full duty. You can do no more. Abandon your cabin. Now it's every man for himself. You look out for yourselves. I release you. That's the way of it at this kind of a time. Every man for himself!'

The two operators, however, continued to send messages as they prepared to switch over to the emergency transmitter. In 'that last awful fifteen minutes,' Bride wrote, his senior colleague carried on sending even as they heard the water rushing over the boat

Left: The ship's orchestra which played on until the end.

Below left: The *Titanic*'s wireless room.

deck. At the last possible moment, as water was pouring through the doorway, Phillips had called out: 'Come, let's clear out.'

By now it was about 2.05 am and all the lifeboats had been lowered. It was only now that the Captain, Wilde, and Murdoch began to lose control of the crowds thronging the decks. They armed themselves with small firearms and, very occasionally, fired into the air.

So far we have scarcely mentioned the passengers in the third and steerage-class accommodation who now began to emerge on deck. One reason for this is that none was called to give evidence at the British inquiry, and none of the survivors wrote an account of the sinking from their own point of view, as did many of those in the first and second classes.

broken down and the stewards dispersed, it is likely that there would still have been sufficient time, had they so wished, for women to make their way on to the boat deck and so into a lifeboat. A Swedish survivor August E Wennerstrom was irritated by what to him seemed the pathetic sight of hundreds of them 'in a circle with a preacher in the middle, praying and crying to God and Mary to help them. . . They just prayed and yelled, never lifting a hand to help themselves.'

The water reached the third-class accommodation in the aft of the ship only late after the collision. This was because, with the bows flooded, the fore section of the ship had settled in the water, lifting the aft clear. Without good communication and a general command of 'abandon ship' those in the lower decks in this section of the ship would have been oblivious to the happenings on deck. It is this failure of communication, as much as any failure on the part of Harland and Wolff to provide for easy third-class access to the lifeboats, which accounts for the high

Left: A dramatic painting of the crowded decks.

Below: The painful farewells.

As we saw, the people in the prow of the vessel had been some of the first to realize that something was amiss. Some of them proceeded to the boat deck and had a good chance of getting away, but many collected their belongings and struggled aft to join their families and friends. Here they remained for a considerable time after the initial collision and it was only after at least an hour had passed that any of them emerged on to the boat deck. Some had been led by stewards via a circuitous route up the staircase to the third-class lounge on C Deck, across the well deck and through the second- and first-class accommodation to the grand staircase leading to the boat deck. Others attempted to find their own way and later told of stewards and even gates blocking their entry into the first- and second-class quarters. Many of the families huddled together in the third-class accommodation aft at a time when they could have been escaping in the lifeboats. It is likely that this behavior, combined with a failure of will to communicate with such a heterogeneous group, explains the low number of female survivors in this class.

Even after the barrier gates had been

casualty rate amongst the third-class passengers.

The boarding of the lifeboats had at first been conducted with the utmost decorum and nicety. As a group of first-class women passengers told the New York Times: 'The whole thing was so formal that it was difficult for anyone to realize that it was a tragedy. It all seemed like a play . . . enacted for entertainment.'

But now, with the steerage and third-class passengers crowding on to the decks, and

with a greatly reduced crew, the officers and men trying to launch the remaining lifeboats were sorely stretched. Only by firing twice into the air did the purser prevent a rush on number 15, and on the port side Lightoller had to evict a number of male stowaways from one of the boats.

It was soon after this incident, and with the *Titanic* sinking fast, that the *Titanic*'s owner, J B Ismay, was assisting the crew in loading up what he assumed to be one of the last Engelhardt collapsibles. As he later told the

Left: The 92-feet drop to the dark ocean. There were eyewitness reports of lifeboats being lowered on top of one another.

Above: One of the *Titanic* myths: Captain Smith shouting 'Be British' as his ship sank.

Right: The eccentric J J Astor, 'the world's greatest monument to unearned increment.'

Senate Inquiry: 'there was a certain number of men in the boat, and the officer called out if there were any more women, and there were no passengers on the deck . . . and as the boat was in the act of being lowered away, I got into it.' Others spoke of Ismay literally being bundled into the boat by Chief Officer Wilde. Although he survived, Ismay was a sad and persecuted man for the rest of his life. Typical of the vitriol which this action provoked was a poem by Ben Hecht which appeared in the *Chicago Journal*

To hold your place in the ghastly face
of death on the sea at night,
Is a seaman's job, but to flee with the mob
Is an owner's noble right.

It was perhaps to escape the mob that T H Andrews of Harland and Wolff stood alone in the smoking room with his eyes fixed on the painting above the Adam-style fireplace. A steward asked him 'aren't you going to have a try for it Mr Andrews?' The latter made no answer but 'just stood like one stunned.' Ironically the painting was entitled *The Approach to the New World*.

Back on the boat deck a small group of millionaires assembled to meet their fate. They included J J Astor, George B Widener, John B Thayer, and Benjamin Guggenheim. Guggenheim and his secretary had changed into evening dress so that they were 'prepared to go down like gentlemen.' While changing, he had told a steward: 'I am willing to remain and play the man's game if there are not enough boats for more than the women and children. I won't die here like a beast. Tell my wife I played the game out straight and to the end. No woman shall be left aboard this ship because Ben Guggenheim is a coward.'

Elsewhere, men were in fact playing real games. After the lifeboat had left the ship,

Messrs Millet, Moore, Butt, and Ryerson had returned to the smoking room where, oblivious to the goings on around them, they played at cards until the end.

Some of the last to emerge from the hold of the ship were the engineers. These heroic officers had labored against increasing odds to man the pumps in the holds of the ship thus keeping her afloat for as long as possible. When they came out on deck the falls hanging from every davit head were empty and all the lifeboats gone. All 35 of them perished.

The *Titanic* was now sinking fast, the water lapping around the bridge. The crowd on deck pushed hopelessly towards the stern; 'a mass of hopeless and dazed humanity, attempting,' in the words of Jack Thayer, 'as the Almighty and Nature made us, to keep our final breath until the last possible moment.'

It was now 2.20 am and some two hours 40 minutes since the *Titanic* had struck the iceberg. 1500 people, mainly men, but a few women crowded the stern of the stricken liner as Lightoller struggled to release the last Engelhardt collapsible. Below them, on the freezing cold sea, bobbed 16 lifeboats, some full and some half empty. From these they could see the massive outline of the *Titanic*, silhouetted against the starlit sky, her blackness emphasized by row upon row of lights still burning. The sea around the *Titanic* was littered with assorted steamer chairs and other wooden debris, thrown overboard in a last desperate attempt to provide for buoyancy in the water.

It was soon after he had released the last of lifeboats that the heroic Lightoller made his miraculous escape from the *Titanic*. Working forward of the passengers huddled on the stern, he found himself being sucked down the forward funnel by an inrush of water. Suddenly a blast of hot air ascended from the bowls of the ship. This was strong enough to

blow him clear of the funnel and toward a nearby Engelhardt lifeboat. The funnel then came crashing down causing both Lightoller and this Engelhardt to be washed to safety, 50 yards clear of the sinking ship. Lightoller was able to scramble on to the upturned Engelhardt. And it was from this precarious perch that he was able to observe the last dreadful moments of the greatest liner the world had ever known:

Slowly and almost majestically the immense stern reared itself up, with propellors and rudders clearing the water, till at last she assumed the exact perpendicular. Then with an ever quickening glide, she slid beneath the water of the cold Atlantic . . . Like a prayer as she disappeared, the words were breathed, 'She's gone.'

Beesley added more detail: 'As she swung up her lights, which had shone without a flicker all night, went out suddenly, came on again for a single flash, then went out altogether.'

It was when the ship swung up that a stupendous explosion emanated from inside her as the boilers and engines came adrift and cracked through the bulkheads. This was soon followed by a sound more terrible still. This was the sound of hundreds of men and women as they wrestled with the freezing water. In the words of John Thayer 'this terrible continuing cry lasted for twenty to thirty minutes, gradually dying away, as one after another could no longer withstand the cold.'

Thayer asked the question of why none of the lifeboats had gone back to rescue those drowning in the water. For although his boat was already full to the gills many others had a considerable surplus capacity. Thayer's question was never satisfactorily answered at either the American or the British inquiry. It seems that in most of the boats either the crew or prominent passengers forbade any attempt to pick up survivors. One of the exceptions was boat #14, under the command

Above: John B Thayer witnessed the *Titanic*'s descent from a collapsible lifeboat. He made these six drawings aboard the *Carpathia*.

59

Right: Captain Smith in the water swims towards an upturned collapsible.

Below: A stylized contemporary painting of the final descent.

of Fifth Officer Lowe. His boat returned to the wreckage where he and his crew 'turned over several [bodies] to see if they were alive.' In the words of one of his seamen, 'It looked as if none of them were drowned. They looked as if frozen.' Lowe rescued at least four people from the water as his boat floated around the debris until daybreak.

Confusion and incomprehension seems to have reigned in the boats. One thing however was apparent: the *Titanic* had not been ringed by safety vessels as her designers had envisaged. However, a boat was visible on the horizon. Number 8 boat, with the Countess Rothes at the tiller, attempted to make for the 'two lights not farther than ten miles off,' but, as a steward said, 'we could not seem to make any headway.' Generally, however, the boats sought to stick together and grimly await a rescue. Fortunately for

Left: The *Titanic*'s lights went out as she sank beneath the glassy sea.

Below: Wireless operator H T Cottam of the *Carpathia* was the first to learn of the *Titanic*'s plight.

them the night was exceptionally clear and the sea like glass.

Morale was lifted from time to time by the occasional quip. Thus a fireman remarked, 'I like a bird that sings in the morning,' as a sea bird flew past. Just over an hour after the *Titanic*'s final descent a far more encouraging sound was heard in the form of a rocket. Some time after this a light and then another was seen rising above the southern horizon. These lights were soon identified as the twin masthead lights of a rescuing vessel. To the accompaniment of the song 'Pull for the shore boys,' #13 lifeboat led the others towards these lights. En route Fifth Officer Lowe spotted 2 Englehardt lifeboats. On one of these he made contact with Second Officer Lightoller but not, alas, with Chief Wireless operator Phillips, who had recently collapsed and died. The living were taken off one of the Englehardts and the other was taken in tow.

THE *CARPATHIA*

The 13,600-ton Cunard liner *Carpathia* had left New York on the same day as the *Titanic* had set out from Queenstown. Cruising at a speed of some 14 knots, she too had received a number of ice warnings on 14 April. Her operator, H T Cottam, had informed Captain Arthur Rostron immediately. Cottam

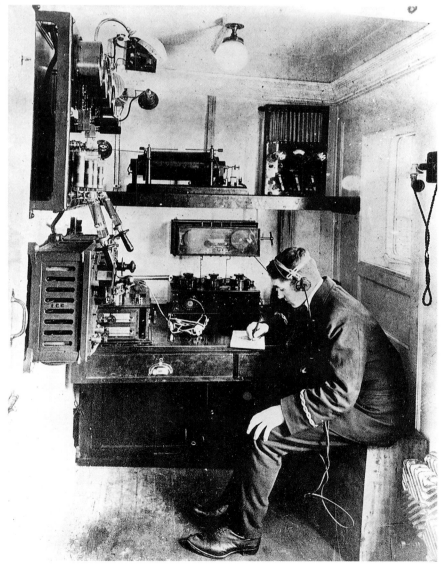

Right and below: Titanic survivors approach the *Carpathia*. Note the varying levels of crowding on the various boats.

seems to have been an exceptionally dedicated operator. For long after he should have gone to bed he was still listening out for news of the coal strike in England. Indeed he was half undressed when he picked up the *Titanic*'s distress signal. This was immediately communicated to his Master and the vessel turned around. Cottam informed the *Titanic* that the *Carpathia* would be able to cover the 58 miles within four hours. No fewer than 14 lookouts were posted on her bows and crow's nest to search for icebergs. She first encountered ice at 2.45 and for the next hour dodged iceberg after iceberg as she made for the *Titanic*'s last stated position. Meanwhile extensive preparations were made for the reception of the survivors.

Shortly before 4 am, as the red rays of dawn began to glow on the eastern horizon, the *Carpathia* was approaching latitude 41° 46′ North, longitude 50° 14′ West. Rostron let off rockets to warn of his imminent arrival. He reduced the *Carpathia*'s speed and steered her towards a green flare visible on the surface of the water. This had been let off by one of the *Titanic*'s lifeboats. As Rostron gently maneuvered his vessel so as to give them a lee, his Second Officer and two quartermasters were sent overside to board the lifeboat. They made the lifeboat fast and maneuvered it to an open side door on C Deck. Two dozen dazed women and ten children were carefully assisted aboard the *Carpathia*. Boxhall the crewmember of the lifeboat was conducted to the bridge. Here the Cunard Captain asked, 'Where is the *Titanic*?' 'Gone. She sank at 2.20 am . . . the other boats are somewhere near' was Boxhall's stark reply.

For the first time Rostron became aware of the magnitude of the situation: at least a thousand people had gone down with the White Star's flagship. He spent the next four hours dodging around icebergs as he picked up survivors from the *Titanic*'s lifeboats. Passengers aboard the *Carpathia* watched in stunned silence as boatload after boatload of survivors either climbed or were hauled aboard. Some were in evening dress, others huddled under overcoats or blankets. Once aboard they were escorted to the dining saloon where hot coffee and sandwiches were awaiting them.

In all, Rostron's vessel had retrieved 706 people that morning. Captain Rostron's prompt action on the night of 14 April and his breakneck dash through the icefield were worthy of the highest traditions of seamanship. The Master of the *Carpathia* was justly praised in the press all over the world.

The behavior of the Master of the *Californian* was rather more controversial. Indeed it still causes considerable rancor even today. Experts might argue over details but certain facts are clear. The 6000-ton *Californian* was bound from London to Boston under the command of Captain Lord when she ran into field ice. Lord hove to and ordered his wireless operator to send out a general ice report at 10.20 pm on 14 April. The *Californian* did not move again until 5.15 the following morning, during which time 1500 had drowned on the *Titanic*.

But that was not all. On the stricken *Titanic* passengers and crew had clearly discerned a steamer at a distance of less than seven miles. Rockets were fired from the *Titanic* and Morse signalling begun. Meanwhile aboard the *Californian* these rockets had been seen at 12.45 am by Stone, her Second Officer. At first Stone thought these to be a shooting star, but later identified them as white rockets. At 1.15 am he spoke down the speaking tube to Captain Lord informing him of the white rockets. Asked whether they were 'private signals' as used by companies for recognition signals, he replied that he did not know. Lord then ordered a young apprentice to contact the steamer by Morse lamp. Between 1.15 am and 2 am the apprentice and Second Officer aboard the *Californian* saw three more rockets but still received no reply by Morse lamp. Indeed they thought the steamer was steaming away to the southwest.

By 2 am only her stern light and a glow at the masthead were visible. The steamer appeared to be moving out of sight. The Captain was awoken by apprentice officer Gibson and informed of the fact that 8 rockets had been seen. Captain Lord enquired of the apprentice: 'are you sure there were no colours in them?' Apprentice officer Gibson replied, 'No. They were all white.' Captain Lord continued to slumber on his couch until he was awoken by his Second Officer who informed him that he could see no more lights and that the ship was out of sight.

At 4 am Second Officer Stone was relieved on the bridge by Chief Officer Stewart. Informed of the events of the last watch,

Left: The *Carpathia* in New York.

Stewart seems to have been alarmed. He woke up Captain Lord and then Evans the wireless operator. After a short delay Evans picked up a message from the Canadian Pacific liner *Mount Temple* that the *Titanic* had struck an iceberg and was sinking. Around 5.15 am the *Californian* set off for the *Titanic*'s last radioed position.

Arriving at the scene at about 8 am the *Carpathia*'s captain semaphored his opposite number aboard the *Californian*, with the awful news, continuing his message: 'I am taking the survivors to New York. Please stay in the vicinity and pick up any bodies.' The *Californian* apparently searched for an hour or so and then continued its passage to Boston. Lord's ship found no bodies and one can only conclude that he did not search very hard since days later the *Halifax* still managed to pick up some two hundred.

Above left: Survivors aboard the *Carpathia*.

Above: Captain Arthur Rostron and his officers.

Left: Crew of the *Titanic* in New York.

THE WORLD REACTS

Above: Crowds gather around the bulletin board of the *New York American.*

NEWS of the *Titanic*'s collision was soon relayed around the world. At first the message was garbled: thus the Evening Star's banner headline announced 'All saved from *Titanic* after collision.' Indeed the owners of the White Star Line – The International Mercantile Marine Company – even issued a statement to the effect that they were absolutely certain that the *Titanic* was able to withstand any damage. The mood of optimism was not to last.

On the morning of 16 April the White Star Line sent the English Board of Trade a brief statement which included the number of passengers picked up. Later that day Prime Minister Asquith addressed a somber House of Commons:

I am afraid we must brace ourselves to confront one of those terrible events in the order of Providence which baffle foresight, which appal the imagination, and which make us feel the inadequacy of words to do justice to what we feel.

In New York the mood of optimism had persisted until about six o'clock in the evening when the *Olympic* sent a (widely intercepted) message to White Star saying that only 675 people had been picked up. Soon the White Star Offices were besieged by an anxious and frantic crowd eagerly awaiting

news. However, the operators aboard the *Carpathia* seemed unable or unwilling to furnish further details, much to the consternation of the world's press; they would have to wait until the *Carpathia* docked for further news.

On the night of 18 April an enormous crowd lined the streets of New York. Their excitement had reached fever heat. As the *Carpathia* entered New York Harbor she was besieged by tugs laden with clamoring reporters. As she docked Marconi (by whose invention so many lives had been saved) came aboard with a reporter from the New York Times. The subsequent interview with

Above: Newspaperboy with tragic placard and (*left*) *New York Times'* front page.

Bride, the *Titanic*'s junior wireless operator, was published later that night in the New York Times. This 'exclusive' represented one of the most important and controversial newspaper scoops of all time. It also established two enduring *Titanic* legends concerning the heroism of Chief Wireless Operator Phillips, in continuing to send out messages and the bravery of the ship's orchestra in continuing to play even as the *Titanic* went down:

The way the band kept playing was a noble thing. . . When I was floating out in the sea with my lifebelt on, it was still on deck playing *Autumn*. How they ever did it I cannot imagine. That and the way Phillips kept sending after the Captain told him his life was his own, and to look out for himself, are two things that stood out in my mind over all the rest.

In England the reporting of the disaster tended to be less anecdotal: 'The *Titanic* like some monstrous syren, had by her beauty and ease, by her splendour and confidence, lured down to the sea men and women to whom life itself seemed subservient and obedient,' wrote the London *Daily Mail*.

Above: Collection in aid of *Titanic* relief fund.

Left: J Bruce Ismay (with umbrella) arriving in Liverpool.

One of the survivors, John Thayer, wrote of the pre-*Titanic* era that 'the world had an even tenor to its ways . . . the disaster . . . was the event which not only made the world rub its eyes and awake, but woke it with a start.' Man had overreached himself.

THE ENQUIRIES

The *Titanic* had been American-owned and went down with a number of prominent Americans on board. Indeed the news was so shocking to the American Senate and people that, even before the survivors had reached New York, an official announcement came from Washington that a special sub-commit-

Above: Lord Mayor of London's collection.

Right: English boyscouts' collection for the families of the victims.

tee was to be set up by the Senate to inquire into the circumstances of the disaster. This enquiry was to be headed by Senator William Smith already well known for his pugnacious and populist style.

Smith began as he meant to continue, issuing subpoenas to prevent the owner and crew of the *Titanic* from leaving America until they had made 'certain explanations to the American people.' Smith began his inquiries first in New York and then in Washington. His enquiry concentrated in detail on the circumstances of the disaster and the behavior of certain passengers and crew. As such it was somewhat more anecdotal than the British enquiry which began about a month after the disaster and which concentrated more on technical aspects of the design and construction of the ship.

Smith saw himself as the standard bearer for the common man fighting in the face of the commercial trusts and cartels of the American subcontinent – such as IMM. Although ignorant of nautical matters he made a virtue of this, stating that 'energy is often more desirable than learning.'

The British enquiry was in many ways a more weighty affair. It was conducted on 36 days during the summer of 1912 by Lord Mersey. He was wholly familiar with the shipping business and maritime law and seems to have had no particular axe to grind. His problem was that, conducting an Official Inquiry or 'Formal Investigation into the loss of the SS *Titanic*,' he was bound to come into conflict with the Board of Trade. They had inspected the *Titanic* and found its safety features to be adequate. Mersey did not shy

Right: Captain Rostron and Mrs J J Brown.

Below: Thomas Whiteley, first saloon steward, whose leg was caught as lifeboats were being lowered.

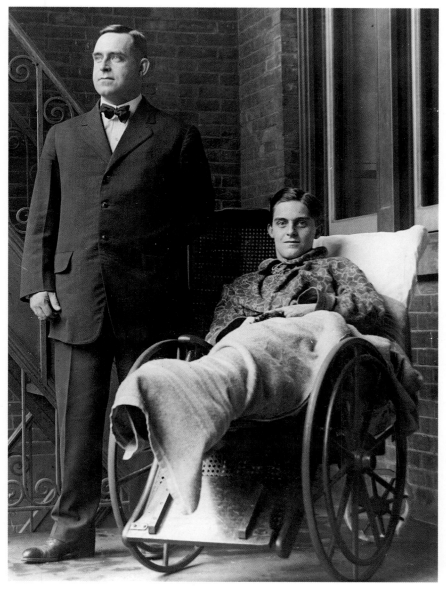

away from criticizing the Board of Trade although he did not charge it with sloth or dereliction of duty – a charge popularly leveled at the Board before the enquiry commenced.

Despite their differences of style and tone, the two enquiries reached similar basic conclusions, though they differed in detail. Thus whereas the American enquiry strongly criticized the insufficient number of lifeboats, the British felt that this obscured the real fundamental design shortcoming; the failure of her designers to carry the bulkheads to a position above the waterline. Both enquiries condemned the prevalent navigational practice of continuing at speed into an area known to contain ice. White Star was however exonerated by the British enquiry since their regulations governing navigational practice cautioned against such conduct. The question of whether or not J B Ismay had prevailed upon Captain Smith to take unnecessary risks was not resolved by Senator Smith and not even addressed by Lord Mersey. Both enquiries agreed that once the ship had been damaged, nothing could have been done to save her. However, more of her passengers could have been saved had the crew been better acquainted with the launching and manning of the lifeboats. Recommendations were made for 24-hour wireless operations on board liners, for more frequent lifeboat drills,

Left: Lord Mersey and his son arrive at the English enquiry.

Right and below: The US enquiry.

Below right: (left to right) Mr Saunderson, General Manager of White Star, and Mr and Mrs J B Ismay arrive at the Court.

and for the steering of a more southerly route across the Atlantic. The American and English enquiries were critical of the mysterious behavior of Captain Lord of the *Californian* for failing to come to the rescue of a stricken vessel – for whatever reasons.

The enquiries differed most widely in their conclusions surrounding the *Titanic*'s master. He had deliberately allowed his vessel to cruise at full speed into an area known to be littered with icebergs. For his part Lord Mersey 'hoped that the last has been heard of the practice. . . What was a mistake in the case of the *Titanic* would without doubt be negligence in any similar case in the future.' His enquiry therefore found Captain Smith not guilty of criminal negligence.

Senator Smith reached a different conclusion: 'Captain Smith knew the sea and his clear eye . . . had often guided his ship through dangerous paths. . . Over-confidence seems to have dulled the faculties usually so alert.' Man had placed too much faith in his own invention until, finally, he had deluded even himself. Perhaps the Bishop of Winchester was right when he referred to the *Titanic* as 'a monument to human presumption.'

THE TITANIC IS FOUND

Left and above: Paris, 1987: TV presentation of 800 *Titanic* artefacts including (left) a whisky bottle.

THE legend of the *Titanic* lived on in memory, folklore, popular song, literature and film – notably *A Night to Remember* based on the book of that name by Walter Lord. Meanwhile the wreck of the sunken vessel rested undisturbed in its dark grave some 2½ miles deep under the North Atlantic. Her last position had been calculated by dead reckoning and was probably accurate only to around a half mile.

It was not, therefore, until the advent of highly sensitive deep water-sonar technology in the late 1970s that any serious attempts could be made to locate the wreck. In the early 1980s three unsuccessful attempts to find the ship had been financed by the Texan oil millionaire Jack Grimm. On the last of his trips he had photographed what

was possibly one of the *Titanic*'s giant propellors. In the summer of 1985, though, a French team on the research ship *Surtoit* used sophisticated side-scanning sonar to locate a massive object on the ocean floor near to the place where the *Titanic* went down.

The French were working with an American team from the Woods Hole Oceanographic Institute directed by *Titanic* expert Dr Robert Ballard. Soon the Americans homed in on the French discovery and, using their new computerized submersibles *Argo* and *Angus*, explored the ocean's depths.

The *Argo*, which was essentially a development for the US Navy, was capable of operating at depths of up to 20,000 feet. Controlled from a control center on the surface, the two submersibles sent back pictures

Above right and right: Two views from Argus with (top) a silver serving platter and (below) the area behind the bridge.

(video in the case of the *Argo*, and stills in that of the *Angus*) via a steel-armored coaxial cable. Descending to a depth of 13,000 feet the *Argo* lived up to its name, for it was on the *Argo* that the Greek hero Jason had searched the world for the Golden Fleece. After a week's unsuccessful searching there suddenly loomed up in the darkness the distinctive outline of a ship's boat deck. The team aboard the control ship *Knorr* held its breath as the *Argo*'s strobe lights revealed the bows of a ship. The *Argo* then edged its way aft passing, as it did so, the empty davits from which a lifeboat had been lowered on that fateful night 73 years earlier. As Ballard said 'suddenly it hit me in the stomach.'

This initial pass over the wreck had lasted only 6 minutes. It had however revealed much useful information: the *Titanic* was upright and a major portion was intact. Some confusion set in after the third run when the *Argo* reached the position where the stern half of the *Titanic*'s hull should have been; the video images faded into a disorientating mass of twisted wreckage. The stern section appeared to have become detached from the rest of the wreck. It was later found at some distance removed from the body of the ship.

As the wind and seas began to rise the *Argo*'s sister sub *Angus* was sent down to collect still shots of the wreck. In all she made six passes over the *Titanic* and when the film was developed Ballard's team found themselves examining a somber collection of photographs of objects of the Edwardian era, strewn across the ocean's floor – a silver serving platter here, a chamber pot there, not to mention numerous unopened bottles of wine. These pictures complemented the video images sent back by the *Argo*, as the Woods Hole team battled against the threatening weather and the ticking of the clock. All too soon it was time to leave. But Ballard's team (minus their French colleagues) returned to the exact position of the site a year later. This time they would have twelve days to explore the wreck and to do so they had brought with them two new subs, *Alvin* and *Jason Junior*.

Alvin was a two-man sub used to hover safely out of danger over the wreck from where her crew could select places for more

detailed examination. Her first descent was largely experimental, but on the second Ballard and his co-pilot Ralph Hollis found themselves confronting for the first time the huge, sharp profile of the *Titanic*'s bow with the anchors still in position. Rivers of rust oozed from the hull on to the ocean bed where she was firmly lodged. For Ballard this was both an exciting and a comforting sight since it was clear that any attempt to raise the hull would be well-nigh impossible. *Alvin* and its two-man crew then moved aft toward the bridge.

On later descents *Jason Junior* was attached to *Alvin*'s underside from where it was deployed to explore deep inside the *Titanic*. Descending the grand staircase – once the

Left: The *Argo* aboard the research vessel *Knorr*.

Above: Robert Ballard and Jean Jarry of the French Sea Rescue Institute.

very hub of the ship – *Jason Junior* sent back spellbinding images of the ship's interior. The *Titanic* had at last yielded up her secrets of 74 years in the form of remarkable pictures of furnishing, chandeliers, heaters, and nameplates.

Their twelve days up, the exploration team returned to Woods Hole with the words 'This is a quiet and peaceful place and a fitting place for the remains of this greatest of sea tragedies to rest.' Others though were less respectful. For with her exact position and condition verified by the scientists at Woods Hole entrepreneurs flocked to the ship raiding it of artefacts sure to raise high prices in the great sale-houses of New York and London. The *Titanic* had been a folly to human grandeur and, perhaps, this was the final ironical twist to her extraordianry story.

Left and below left;
Robert Ballard and
friends.

Right and below:
Anchors, chains,
winches and capstans,
davits, on the hulk of
the *Titanic*

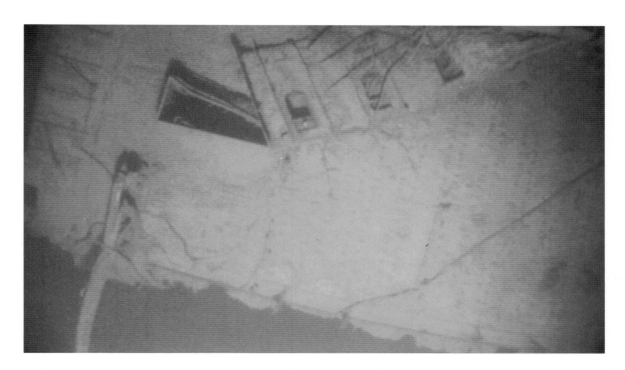

INDEX

ACKNOWLEDGMENTS

Associated Press/Worldwide Photos: pages 52 (below), 66, 74 (all three)

The Bettmann Archive: pages 1, 8, 24 (below), 25 (both), 27 (above left), 38, 39 (above), 44 (both), 48 (above), 53 (below), 54 (above), 56 (above), 58 (below), 58-59 (top), 61 (below), 62-63, 64, 67 (below), 70 (right), 71 (below), 72 (below)

Bettmann/Hulton: page 28 (above), 29 (above), 53 (above), 57, 58 (center), 60 (above), 61 (above), 62, 65 (above left), 67 (above), 68 (above), 69 (above), 70, 72 (above)

Bettmann Archive/Woods Hole Oceanographic Institute: page 75 (both)

The Granger Collection: page 55 (above)

The Mansell Collection: pages 27 (above right), 45, 56 (below)

The National Maritime Museum, Greenwich: pages 2-3

The Titanic Historical Society, Inc, Indian Orchard, MA; pages 6 (above), 7 (all three), 11, 12 (below), 13, 14 (above right and below right), 15 (above), 15 (below, George Behe Collection), 16-17 (above and below), 19, 21, 22, 23 (both), 24 (above), 27 (below), 29 (below), 30 (above), 31 (above), 33, 34 (George Behe Collection), 35 (top), 36, 37 (George Behe Collection), 39 (below), 40 (National Maritime Museum, London), 41 (both), 43 (all five; top left: Ray Lepian Collection), 44 (above), 46-47, 48 (left), 49, 50 (both), 51, 52 (above), 54 (below), 55 (below), 71 (right)

The Ulster Folk and Transport Museum, Cultra Manor, Holywood, Co. Down: pages 4-5, 7 (below), 9 (Harland and Wolff Collection), 10, 14 (above left), 18-19 (above), 18-19 (below: Harland and Wolff Collection), 30 (below), 32 (above), 35 (center and bottom), 36 (left), 42, 47

UPI/Bettmann: pages 12 (above), 17, 20-21, 26, 28 (below), 60 (below), 65 (above right and below), 73 (both), 76, 77